S0-BBF-071

Barbette Spaeth

Luciana Jacobelli

GLADIATORS AT POMPEII

The J. Paul Getty Museum
Los Angeles

Italian edition © 2003 "L'ERMA" di BRETSCHNEIDER

First published in the United States of America in 2003 by
Getty Publications
1200 Getty Center Drive, Suite 500
Los Angeles, California 90049-1682
www.getty.edu

English translation © 2003 J. Paul Getty Trust

Christopher Hudson, *Publisher*
Mark Greenberg, *Editor in Chief*
Robin H. Ray, *Copy Editor*
Mary Becker, *Translator*
Diane L. Franco, *Typesetter*

Giovanni Portieri, *Graphic Designer*
Maurizio Pinto, *Computer Layout and Pagination*

Photographic credits:
Foto Studio Foglia
Archaeological Superintendence of Pompeii
L. Jacobelli
Archaeological Institute Germanico
Musee de la Civilisation Gallo-Romaine de Lyon

Printed in Italy by «L'ERMA» di BRETSCHNEIDER

Library of Congress Cataloging-in-Publication Data

Jacobelli, Luciana.
    [Gladiatori a Pompeii. English]
    Gladiators at Pompeii / Luciana Jacobelli ; introduction by Riccardo
Lattuada.
        p. cm.
Includes bibliographical references and index.
    ISBN 0-89236-731-8 (hardcover)
    1. Gladiators in art. 2. Art, Roman—Italy—Pompeii (Extinct city)
3. Games—Italy—Pompeii (Extinct city)—History. I. Title.
N8217.G5J3313 2003
704.9'423'09377—dc22

                                2003019057

Contents

To Aunt Vittoria and to "the Red"

PART ONE

THE INSTITUTION
OF GLADIATORIAL COMBAT
Its Origins and Evolution

The many theories concerning the origins of gladiatorial games boil down essentially to two: one dates them back to the Etruscans, the other traces the games to the Oscan-Lucanians. The theory of an Etruscan origin is based essentially on literary sources (Athenaeus *Deipnosophistai* 4.153; Tertullian *Ad nationes* 1.10.47, *Apologeticum* 15.5; Isidore of Seville *Origines* 10.159), though at present archaeological data to support this thesis is lacking. Given what we know to date, the second theory, placing the origin of the games in the Oscan-Lucanian environment, prevails. Indeed, the very oldest depictions of gladiatorial combat, discovered in painted tombs in Capua and Paestum and dating back to the fourth century B.C., come from this area (FIGURE 1). They are scenes of duels, boxing, and chariot races—allusions

FIGURE 1.
Tomb plaque from the necropolis in Laghetto, with scene of a duel (4th century B.C.). Paestum, Museo Archeologico (inv. 5014).

to the games held during the funerals of prominent local figures. Some vases from the same period, decorated with scenes of duels, also come from this area. Together with the paintings, they establish the most direct antecedents of gladiatorial combat.

Originally, gladiatorial games were linked to funeral rites. They were a kind of tribute made to the deceased, from which derives the name used in antiquity: "*munus*," meaning "duty" or "gift." On the basis of later sources (Tertullian *De spectaculis* 12), some scholars have hypothesized that the victim's blood was an offering intended to placate the dead. It has also been seen as a reflection of the ancient rites of human sacrifice presumed to have taken place at funerals.

In Rome, too, the advent of gladiatorial combat was tied to funeral rites. The first gladiatorial spectacle was given in the Forum Boarium in 264 B.C. for the funeral of Giunius Brutus Pera (Valerius Maximus 2.4–7; Livy *Periochae* 16). From then on, gladiatorial contests became widespread at the funeral rites of the Romans. It was not uncommon for someone to specify his own funeral arrangements in his will, instructing his heir to offer games that would perpetuate his memory and render the ceremony unforgettable (Seneca *De brevitate vitae* 20.6; Dio Cassius 37.51). But early on, the *munera* began to change, losing their original ceremonial and funereal character to become, increasingly, spectacles in their own right.

In 105 B.C. the consuls P. Rutilius Rufus and Cn. Manlius Maximus organized, for the very first time, a contest without any link to a specific occasion, thereby inaugurating a series of public entertainments (Valerius Maximus 2.3.2). Thenceforward, the games became an indispensable means for career politicians to gain fame and popularity. The *munera gladiatoria* were so popular with the spectators—composed in good part of voters—that a magistrate who was particularly generous in offering a spectacle was guaranteed reelection. For this reason, the games became more and more costly and elaborate towards the end of the Republic. These excesses prompted a law (*lex Tullia de ambitu*) that prohibited public figures from offering gladiatorial spectacles in the two years preceding their election to public office (Cicero *In Vatinium* 15.37).

On the other hand, by the end of the Augustan reign, it had become obligatory for magistrates to offer a spectacle during their tenure, on a date established by the city council. The expenses fell partly on the magistrate and partly on the city, but sometimes the magistrate, in an act of magnanimity, would refuse public aid and pay for the show entirely out of his own purse.

The gladiatorial entertainments were also an important means of political propaganda for the emperor, who knew that they would both increase his popularity and appease the turbulent populace. It was the poet Juvenal (*Saturae* 10.81) who coined the phrase "*panem et circenses*" ("bread and circuses") to stigmatize the politics of consensus practiced by the Roman emperors in the face of their subjects. The gladiatorial entertainments lasted until the fifth century A.D., when they were officially abolished. The *venationes*, or hunts, lasted up until the sixth century.

TYPES OF GLADIATORS

During the Republic, the armor worn by gladiators was very similar to military armor. After the reform enacted by the emperor Augustus, gladiators were divided into various categories based on their type of armor and their style of fighting. No clear iconographic equivalents have been found for all the gladiator types cited in the literary and epigraphic sources. Therefore we can't give very detailed descriptions of the paraphernalia worn by certain types of fighters or their opponents. Some scholars even express doubt and difference of opinion when it comes to identifying some of the better-known types. What follows are the most recent and widely shared hypotheses on the identity and paraphernalia of the most famous and best-documented categories of gladiators, particularly in Pompeii.

1. The Samnites

The Samnites (*Samnes*) are the oldest of the gladiatorial types known to us. According to Livy (9.40), in 309 B.C. the Samnites, who originated from present-day Sannio and Molise, experienced a harsh defeat at the hands of the Romans. The Campanians, who were allies of the Romans, were able to get a share of the splendid arms that the Samnites had left behind on the battlefield. With these arms they outfitted the gladiators, who then assumed the name "Samnites" (FIGURE 2).

The Samnite was heavily armed. He had a very large round or rectangular shield (*scutum*), a leather legging on his left leg, sometimes trimmed with metal, and a short sword with a straight, pointed blade (*gladius*), or a lance. He was protected by a helmet that had both a visor and a crest and was decorated with feathers (*galea*). Under Augustus, the Samnite became obsolete as a type of gladiator, because it would have been offensive to the Samnites, now allies of the Romans, to feature him in the arena. He was replaced by two new types: the *secutor* and the *hoplomachus*, or as some scholars believe, the *secutor* and the *murmillo*.

FIGURE 2.
Red-figure amphora with a Samnite warrior (4th century B.C.). Naples, Museo Archeologico Nazionale (inv. 82744).

2. The *Hoplomachus*

This type of gladiator is not easy to identify because his armor was similar to the Thracian's (see below). He wore high leggings and an impressive helmet decorated with feathers and an upturned brim. As with the Thracian, horizontal bandages over the thighs sometimes appear in the images of the *hoplomachus* (FIGURE 3). But he is distinguished by his straight sword, his plain helmet, and his rather small, round shield. His opponent was either a Thracian or a *murmillo*.

FIGURE 3, OPPOSITE
Detail of Pompeian marble relief showing a contest between a *hoplomachus* and a *murmillo* (A.D. 20–50). Naples, Museo Archeologico Nazionale (inv. 6704).

FIGURE 4.
Leggings worn by a *Thraex* (1st century A.D.). Naples, Museo Archeologico Nazionale (inv. 5666–67).

FIGURE 5.
Stone relief showing combat between a Thracian and a gladiator with heavy armor. The victor is the Thracian holding the curved dagger (*sica*), ready for the final thrust (1st century A.D.). Sepino, Antiquarium.

3. The Thracian

Like the Samnites and the Gauls (on the latter we have very little information), the Thracian (*Thraex*) derives his name from the warriors of Thrace (modern-day Bulgaria), with whom the Romans came into contact at the time of the wars against Mithridates. The Thracian's armor included a small, strongly convex, squarish shield (*parmula*), a *manica* (armband) on the right arm, and two high leggings, often decorated up to the knee (FIGURE 4). The weapon most typical of this gladiator was a short sword, either curved or angled, called a *sica* (FIGURE 5). Even his helmet was unusual: it was generally topped with a tall crest decorated with the relief of

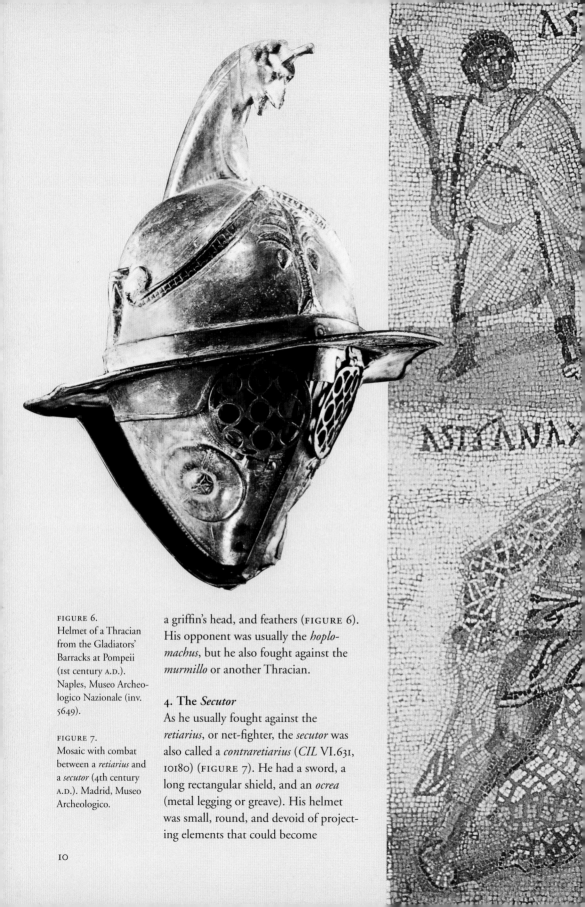

FIGURE 6.
Helmet of a Thracian
from the Gladiators'
Barracks at Pompeii
(1st century A.D.).
Naples, Museo Archeo-
logico Nazionale (inv.
5649).

FIGURE 7.
Mosaic with combat
between a *retiarius* and
a *secutor* (4th century
A.D.). Madrid, Museo
Archeologico.

a griffin's head, and feathers (FIGURE 6).
His opponent was usually the *hoplomachus*, but he also fought against the
murmillo or another Thracian.

4. The *Secutor*
As he usually fought against the
retiarius, or net-fighter, the *secutor* was
also called a *contraretiarius* (*CIL* VI.631,
10180) (FIGURE 7). He had a sword, a
long rectangular shield, and an *ocrea*
(metal legging or greave). His helmet
was small, round, and devoid of project-
ing elements that could become

ensnared in his opponent's net (FIGURE 8). The helmet was completely closed in front, with small holes for the eyes. This gladiator's fighting strategy was to get close to his opponent, using his shield for protection. His opponent, on the other hand, tried to avoid fighting up close because his own weapons, the net and the trident, were effective only if deployed from a distance. For his own part, the *secutor* had everything to gain from moving in as quickly as possible, because with his heavy armor and the limited amount of air in his helmet, he tired out sooner than his opponent.

FIGURE 8, OPPOSITE
Bronze statuette of a
secutor with a helmet
that opens to show the
gladiator's face (2nd
century A.D.). Musée
de l'Arles Antiques.

FIGURE 9.
Drawing of two net-
fighters from the deco-
ration on the podium
of the Pompeian
amphitheater, now
lost (ADS 88).

5. The *Retiarius*

This gladiator, with his net and trident, is easy to recognize. With a technique that may have been inspired by fishermen, he attempted to wrap his opponent in his net, rendering him powerless. A trident and a short sword were his weapons. If he lost the net, he could use his trident to land a two-handed blow on his opponent (FIGURE 7). The net-fighter's costume was similar to that of other gladiators, with a few differences. Like others, he wore the *subligaculum*—a loincloth tied to his belt (*balteus*). Yet, unlike other gladiators, he wore a *manica* on his left arm (not his right) to more successfully maneuver the net (FIGURE 9). Completely unique to the net-fighter was the *galerus*, a rectangular plate of bronze foil tied to his left shoulder, rising up about twelve or thirteen centimeters to protect his bare head. During the excavation of the

FIGURE 10.
Galerus found in the
Gladiators' Barracks
at Pompeii on January
10, 1767. The decora-
tion in relief includes
a rudder, an anchor,
a crab, and a trident
with a dolphin (1st
century A.D.). Naples,
Museo Archeologico
Nazionale (inv. 5639).

FIGURE 11.
Legging of a *murmillo*
from Pompeii, deco-
rated with a victorious
gladiator holding a
palm branch. Naples,
Museo Archeologico
Nazionale (inv. 5663).

quadriporticus of the theaters at
Pompeii, three different specimens of
galerus were found. One was decorated
with marine symbols (FIGURE 10);
another with a relief of Hercules' head
and some cupids; and a third with an
engraving of the net-fighter's weapons
and the abbreviation "RET / SECUND"
("*Retiarius*, second rank") accompanied
by a palm and a crown, the symbols of
victory. These pieces vary in size from
thirty to thirty-five centimeters in width
and height and weigh about one kilo.
The *retiarius* was also matched against
the *murmillo*.

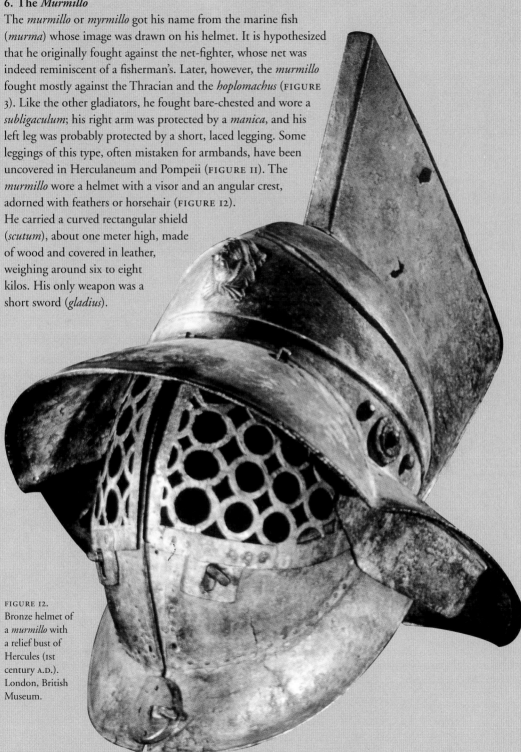

6. The *Murmillo*

The *murmillo* or *myrmillo* got his name from the marine fish
(*murma*) whose image was drawn on his helmet. It is hypothesized
that he originally fought against the net-fighter, whose net was
indeed reminiscent of a fisherman's. Later, however, the *murmillo*
fought mostly against the Thracian and the *hoplomachus* (FIGURE
3). Like the other gladiators, he fought bare-chested and wore a
subligaculum; his right arm was protected by a *manica*, and his
left leg was probably protected by a short, laced legging. Some
leggings of this type, often mistaken for armbands, have been
uncovered in Herculaneum and Pompeii (FIGURE 11). The
murmillo wore a helmet with a visor and an angular crest,
adorned with feathers or horsehair (FIGURE 12).
He carried a curved rectangular shield
(*scutum*), about one meter high, made
of wood and covered in leather,
weighing around six to eight
kilos. His only weapon was a
short sword (*gladius*).

FIGURE 12.
Bronze helmet of
a *murmillo* with
a relief bust of
Hercules (1st
century A.D.).
London, British
Museum.

FIGURE 13.
Marble relief with two gladiators, probably *provocatores*, in combat on the left. Rome, Museo Nazionale Romano (inv. 126119).

FIGURE 14.
Terra-cotta tile ("lastra Campana") with scene of a *venatio* (1st century A.D.). Rome, Museo Nazionale Romano (inv. 62660).

62660

7. The *Provocator*

Though the *provocator* was already known in Cicero's time (*Pro Sestio* 64), we don't have much specific information about him. He wore a *subligaculum* and had some protection halfway up his left leg. He wore a helmet with a visor but no crest and bore a curved rectangular shield. He also carried a kind of cuirass to protect his chest (FIGURE 13). Usually, *provocatores* fought against other *provocatores*. With weapons and armor weighing a total of around fourteen to fifteen kilos, this could be considered a middleweight category.

8. The *Eques*

The *eques* was a gladiator who fought on horseback. He wore a helmet with a visor, a short tunic, and bands to protect his thighs and his right arm. He was armed with a lance and a small round shield (*parma equestris*), and he fought only against other *equites*. In reliefs, the *eques* was often depicted without his horse, probably because his match ended in hand-to-hand combat with a sword.

9. Other Gladiators

There were other types of gladiators about whom less is known: the *essedarius* fought on top of a cart; the *dimachaerus* was probably armed with two daggers; the *veles* fought with a javelin and a strap (*hasta amentata*).

Finally, there were the *venatores* and the *bestiarii*, who fought against wild beasts in spectacular hunting shows (*venationes*) (FIGURE 14). They wore short tunics and were armed with *venabuli*, wooden spits or poles with iron tips, and leather whips. Sometimes the *venator* is depicted with a cap-shaped helmet, *ocreae*, and a small straight sword.

FEMALE GLADIATORS

Some ancient sources refer to the participation of women in the amphitheater games during the reign of Nero. Tacitus (*Annales* 15.32–33) reports that during a splendid show in A.D. 63, some noblewomen and senators even entered the arena to fight. In A.D. 66, at the *munus* offered in Pozzuoli by Nero in honor of Tiridates, the king of Armenia, Ethiopian women were introduced into the arena (Dio Cassius 62.3.1). The satirical poet Juvenal tells of a certain Mevia, who hunted boars in the arena "with spear in hand and breasts exposed" (*Saturae* 1.22–23). In his famous sixth satire against women, Juvenal gives an

FIGURE 15.
Relief from
Halicarnassus with
female gladiators in
combat (2nd century
A.D.). London, British
Museum (inv. GR 1847,
4-24-19).

ironic view of the mania that many Roman ladies felt for the arena games
(*Saturae* 6.255–58):

> What a fine thing for a husband, at an auction of his wife's effects, to see
> her belt and armlets and plumes put up for sale, with a gaiter that covers half
> the left leg; or if she fight another sort of battle, how charmed you will be to
> see your young wife disposing of her greaves!

In the *Satyricon* we hear of a *munus* organized by a certain Titus, who went
so far as to present a woman fighting on a cart (Petronius *Satyricon* 45.7). At
the inauguration of the Colosseum, some women participated in the hunts of
wild beasts (Martial *Liber spectaculorum* 6; Dio Cassius 66.25.1). Even under
Domitian, probably in A.D. 89, a *munus* was held at which there were female
gladiators (Dio Cassius 67.8.4; Suetonius *Domitianus* 4.2; Statius *Silvae* 1.8,
51–56). Although there is not much archaeological evidence of female gladiators, a depiction of two women fighting appears on a marble relief from
Halicarnassus (Asia Minor), dating to the second century A.D. (FIGURE 15).
Even their obviously fictional names—Amazon and Achilla—are recorded.

In an epigraph at Ostia, from the second century A.D., a member of the
local elite is extolled as being the first in the history of that city's games to "arm
women." Yet it seems that in A.D. 200 the emperor Septimius Severus put an
end to contests between women in the arena (Dio Cassius 75.16).

SPONSORING AND STAFFING
A GLADIATORIAL SPECTACLE

The complex organization of the gladiatorial spectacles was regulated by special laws (*leges gladiatoriae*), which varied from city to city. The one principle common to all was that no *munera* could be organized without the consent of the emperor or the civil authorities.

Private citizens or magistrates could call a contest for various reasons: to commemorate a deceased member of the family, to celebrate the inauguration of a public monument, on the occasion of a military victory, in honor of the emperor and the imperial family, or to gain favor in the eyes of the people. Furthermore, the local magistrates were expected to offer spectacles, or to carry out public works during their year in office. The sponsor in charge of financing the show was the *editor*.

To organize a spectacle, the *editor* had to employ the services of a *lanista*, who was a professional entrepreneur. The *lanista* bought, sold, and rented his gladiators to whomever wished to sponsor a *munus*. Such a profession could make one rich, but it was always regarded publicly as a disgraceful job. The *lanista* was considered a vendor of human flesh (the word has the same etymological root as the word "*lanius*," or "butcher"), and he was compared to a pimp who exploited prostitutes. The *lanista* kept his troupe of gladiators in special schools (*ludi*), where they were subjected to very strict discipline. To stay in optimal shape for fighting, they trained daily, followed a diet aimed at increasing their muscle mass and weight, and underwent medical checkups. However, the market price of a gladiator depended on his success in the arena, and the agents charged such high rates for the best fighters that, under the emperor Marcus Aurelius, it became necessary to set a cap on spending for each event, and for each gladiator.

Among the oldest and most renowned schools was the one at Capua, from whence erupted the revolt of Spartacus in 73 B.C. (see page 28). The prominent role played by this city in the training of gladiators continued into the Empire. Caesar owned a *ludus* with five thousand gladiators at Capua, and this was, perhaps, the nucleus of the famous *Ludus Iulianus*, the imperial school that would be called the *Ludus Neronianus* under Nero.

Though it was hard, life in the *ludus* was certainly not the equivalent of life imprisonment. The gladiators could come and go freely, and some, like Spartacus, shared their barracks with a female companion (*ludia*). It may be that some gladiators lived in private houses, going to the school only to train. In fact, many of them had families, as evidenced by the sepulchral epigraphs paid for by their wives (FIGURE 16). This was the case for the

FIGURE 16.
Funerary epigraph of two net-fighters, Purpurius and Philematius. The latter died at the age of 30 and was grieved by his wife, Aurelia Aphrodites. Benevento, Museo del Sannio (inv. 1777?).

secutor Urbicus, who died at the age of twenty-two after thirteen fights and seven years of marriage (*CIL* V.5933), or the *retiarius* Iantinus, who died at the age of twenty-four after five fights and five years of marriage (*CIL* V.4506).

Most of the gladiators were prisoners-of-war and slaves earmarked by their owners for a gladiatorial career. Some were criminals who were condemned to death (*noxi ad gladium damnati*) or to forced labor; the latter could be compelled to work off their sentences as gladiators. A considerable difference separated the two categories: the slaves destined to become gladiators did not go directly from prison to the amphitheater like those condemned to death, but were sent to a school to learn how to handle weapons. Furthermore, while those with death sentences had no chance of leaving the arena alive, the slaves had the same chance as any regular gladiator.

Contrary to what many believe, the gladiatorial game was not necessarily meant to end in death, especially since the training of a gladiator was so expensive. Death could result either from the wounds a gladiator received in combat, or when the *editor* or the crowd refused to spare a wounded gladiator. But the latter scenario occurred only when the gladiator failed to carry out his task fully, or to truly engage in the contest. The *editor*, however, was obliged to pay the *lanista* the price for the gladiators whom he had refused to spare. This helps to clarify why there were also freedmen (slaves who had obtained their freedom) and free men—some even from good families—who signed up to fight voluntarily. The free men who dedicated themselves to a gladiatorial career (called *auctorati*) entered into a condition of partial servitude to the *lanista*, and while this didn't compromise their freedom or their citizenship, it did limit their legal eligibility. More often than not, these men were pushed into the profession out of material need, perhaps because they had completely dissipated all of their means (Horace *Epistulae* 1.18.36). But there were others who actually aspired to fame and fortune (Tertullian *Ad martyras* 5). The allure of the gladiatorial profession led even some members of the equestrian and senatorial classes to give up their standing and enter the arena (Tacitus *Annales* 14.14, 15.32; Juvenal 2.143–48; Suetonius *Caesar* 39, *Tiberius* 35, *Nero* 12; Dio Cassius 47.43.3, 51.22.4, 56.25.7–8, 59.13, 61.17). Some emperors promulgated laws in order to contain this phenomenon, but without much success.

Slaves, freedmen, and free men could all be part of the same *familia gladiatoria*, but the documents available to us shed no light on the numbers in question. Certainly the majority of the gladiators were slaves. For one particular show at Pompeii, there appear to have been nineteen slaves and six free men (*CIL* IV.2508); elsewhere, six out of twenty gladiators were free men (*CIL* IX.466). We don't know how long a slave was expected to serve, nor how many times he had to fight before gaining his freedom. However, at the end of his career, a gladiator would receive a *rudis*, or wooden sword, to symbolize his service. Often the *rudiarii* (these "retired" gladiators) would end up as trainers in the gladiatorial schools.

But what kind of a reputation did the gladiators enjoy in civil society? The answer is not simple, and not without contradictions. Gladiators and *bestiarii* who were free men were considered *infames* (Calpurnius Flaccus *Declamationes*

52), and this condition brought with it a series of prohibitions. They were, of course, excluded from the Senate and the equestrian class. Yet, once in a while, the emperor would exonerate some of the gladiators—from these two classes only—of this *infamia*, if they had participated in some special *munera* at his own request.

The gladiator who was formerly a slave, but now a freedman, could not become a Roman citizen, and thus was an *infamis*. Such infamy was tied primarily to the blemish that attached to any actor who made a living doing public performances. It was compounded by the horror that the gladiators' bloodthirstiness and brutality inspired, and their constant contact with death.

Even so, the opposite attitude was present as well: the gladiator was the sweetheart of the crowd, exalted by poets (Martial 5.24); immortalized on vases (FIGURE 17), cups, lamps, frescoes, and simple graffiti; and idolized by women. Juvenal recounts the story of Eppia, the wife of a senator, who abandoned her husband, children, and domestic comforts to follow the gladiator Sergio:

FIGURE 17. Goblet "d'Aco" with a scene of gladiatorial combat. Lyons, Musée de la civilisation Gallo-Romaine.

> And what were the youthful charms that captivated Eppia? What did she see in him to allow herself to be called a "she-Gladiator"? Her dear Sergius had already begun to shave [meaning he was over forty years old]; a wounded arm gave promise of a discharge, and there were sundry deformities in his face: a scar caused by the helmet, a huge bulging nose, and a nasty humor always trickling from his eye. But then he was a gladiator! It is this that transforms these fellows into Hyacinths! (Juvenal Saturae 6.82–113)

Their high public esteem, as well as the regard of some emperors, derived from the fact that the gladiator was seen, above all, as a man of courage, who was continually challenged by death. Even Cicero, who often denigrated his adversaries by calling them gladiators, could not fail to recognize these talents (Cicero *Tusculanae disputationes* 2.17.41). And Seneca returns time and again to the courage of the gladiators (Seneca *De providentia* 3.4, *De costantia sapientis* 16.2). And so, just as their own image was ambiguous, the arena fighters were met with a marked ambivalence in the social realm. The gladiator was both a hero and a murderer, regarded with admiration in one role and horror in the other.

FIGURE 18.
Detail from a relief of
a parade entering the
arena (*pompa*) (A.D.
20–50). Naples, Museo
Archeologico Nazionale
(inv. 6704).

THE SPECTACLE FROM START TO FINISH

The gladiatorial entertainments were announced by means of programs written on the walls of the city buildings (*edicta munerum*) and pamphlets sold in the street (*libelli munerari*), to be consulted later during the show itself (Ovid *Ars amatoria* 1.167). These programs described the reason for the feast day, the name of the games' organizer, the names of the gladiators who would fight that day, and their specialties. Sometimes other bits of information were given in the programs (including the ones posted on the walls). For instance, a velarium might be present to protect the spectators from the sun, or there might be *sparsiones*, which some scholars believe were small favors but which others think were light sprays of perfumed water to alleviate the heat.

FIGURE 19.
Relief of a horn
player (DAIR 958).
Isernia, Antiquarium
comunale.

Usually an amphitheater show began with wild animal fights in the morning and then proceeded with the much-anticipated combat between gladiators in the afternoon. First there was a *pompa*, the official parade of all the players in the show, who were dressed for the occasion in ornate costumes (FIGURE 18). Musicians also participated in the procession with their various instruments: the *tuba* (a wind instrument widely used in the army), the *lituus* (made of a long, slender, bronze pipe, its end recurved), the *cornus* (a bronze wind instrument, originally derived from the horn of an animal; FIGURE 19), the *tibia* (a wind instrument made from reeds of different lengths), and, finally, a kind of organ, which is depicted in the mosaic of Zliten in Tripoli (FIGURE 20).

FIGURE 20.
Mosaic from Zliten depicting the orchestra at a gladiatorial spectacle, including an organist (around A.D. 200). Tripoli, Archeological Museum.

The actual fights were preceded by warm-up exercises, which both heightened the anticipation of the public and displayed the abilities of the gladiators. Before the beginning of the contest, the weapons were examined by the *editor muneris* to see that they met specifications and that no gladiator would be shielded from death because of a feeble weapon. This check was called the *probatio armorum*. Then the chorus of instruments would signal the beginning of the contest, and the gladiators would fight in pairs (usually there were twenty pairs), assisted by the arena personnel: *doctores*, *harenari*, or *incitatores* (FIGURE 18).

The public participated actively. Spectators might spur on a well-known gladiator, give helpful signals, and place bets on individual combatants. If he were wounded, a gladiator could withdraw from the fight and ask for mercy (*missum*). In this case, he would lower his weapons and raise the index finger of his left hand, or else cross his hands behind him in a sign of surrender (FIGURE 21).

The decision to spare a gladiator was left to the *editor*—in some cases, *editor* and emperor were one and the same—but it was customary to take into account the noisily expressed opinion of the crowd. If they had decided that the gladiator should leave the arena alive, the spectators would raise their index fingers or wave their handkerchiefs, yelling "*missum*" ("spare him"). But if they had decided for death, they would stick their thumbs down (*pollicem vertere*), forcing the gladiator to surrender to a mortal blow.

A corps of gladiators, the *supposticii*, stood in reserve, ready to take over for combatants who had been killed or were wounded beyond all hope of

finishing a contest. Often a fight would continue with no clear victor, and in such cases, both gladiators were let go. But there were also special *munera sine missione*, in which the *editor* would refuse to spare any of the defeated gladiators. Dead gladiators were carried out of the arena through the *Porta Libitinensis*, named after Libitina, the goddess of burial, and from thence they were taken to the *spoliarium* to be stripped of their armor.

The winner received the victory palm, which he waved at the crowd while taking a turn around the arena. Each victory brought another palm, and a gladiator kept track of his successes by the number of palms he had received. Furthermore, alongside the honors and glory he enjoyed, a successful gladiator could get rich. The payment, which was established beforehand and was included in the "rental" agreement, was made by the *editor* to the gladiator, who was entitled to keep the money even if he were a slave. Sometimes the sums earned were considerable. The gladiator was paid in the amphitheater right in front of the crowd, and the spectators would count out the coins on their fingers as he received them (Suetonius *Claudius* 21). The coins were handed over on plates of precious metal, which were also given to the victor (Juvenal 6.204; FIGURE 22). The victor might receive ornate weapons and other precious objects as well.

FIGURE 22.
Detail from a mosaic in the vestibule of Eros and Pan, depicting the gifts for the victors: palm branches and bags of money, under the table. Piazza Armerina, Villa del Casale.

Generally the contest ended at dusk, but the show could also run into the night in the torch-lit amphitheater (Suetonius *Domitianus* 4; Dio Cassius 67.8). The results were then made public with an initial beside the name of each gladiator: "P(*erit*)" for dead, "M(*issus*)" for free, or "V(*icit*)" for victor (FIGURES 41–43).

The *venationes* (hunts) took place in the morning. Here, the *venatores* (hunters) would fight against wild animals, or animals would fight each other (FIGURE 23). The variety of animals to hunt in the amphitheater increased over time: in addition to the lions and panthers that made their first appearance in 186 B.C., hippopotamuses, crocodiles, rhinoceroses, bulls, bears, and elephants were introduced into the arena (Livy 39.22.2, 44.18.8). These shows were usually put on to enhance the games, but they were not mandatory. Both literary and iconographic sources confirm that the *venationes* comprised not only animals fighting animals and men fighting animals but also acrobatic exhibitions and games. Such performances surely would have required a long period of training for the animals.

THE AMPHITHEATERS

Initially the contests took place in the forums or "piazzas" of the city (Suetonius *Caesar* 39, *Tiberius* 7). Later, the greater frequency and length of the games led to the construction of special buildings large enough to hold hunts and fights simultaneously. Thus the amphitheater was created. A building typically Roman in style, it consisted in joining together two facing theaters (Ovid *Metamorphoses* 11.25; Isidore of Seville *Origines* 15.2.35).

FIGURE 23.
Gladiators in combat against wild beasts on a mosaic (4th century A.D.). Rome, Galleria Borghese.

FIGURE 24.
Rome, The Colosseum.

THE REVOLT OF SPARTACUS

Of all the great slave insurrections, the one carried off by Spartacus remains the most famous, and it has inspired both novelists and film directors. In antiquity, however, his reputation was mixed. On the one hand, he was considered an outlaw, and on the other, a figure of great stature and exemplary virtue.

The revolt broke out in 73 B.C. in the gladiatorial school of Lentulus Baitatus in Capua. The sources that refer to this episode (especially Plutarch *Life of Crassus* 8–11; Appianos *Bellum civile* 1.116–21; Florus *Epitomae* 2.8) make no mention of the slaves' ideology, but the revolt was probably sparked by prison conditions and the prospect of an uncertain and violent future that these men faced. About seventy slaves, mostly Gauls and Thracians, took the initiative. They managed to flee with some knives and spits taken from the kitchen. Later, they stole gladiatorial weapons from a cart during transport. The slaves succeeded in taking refuge on Vesuvius, where they were joined by some free-men farmers. An army of 3,000 men under the command of C. Claudius Glabrus was sent from Rome to lay siege to the rebels on the mountain. The soldiers blocked the only passage by which the rebels could have freed themselves from the army's grip. But their leader, Spartacus, had them fashion ladders from wild vines and then lower their comrades one by one from the crag of the mountain until they were able to surround and disperse the Roman troops. Other troops sent from Rome were also decimated and defeated.

Spartacus's plan was to march towards the north and across the Alps, returning to Thrace and Gaul, where most of the slaves came from. But the ex-gladiators preferred to linger in the areas around Nola, Nuceria, Eboli, Cosenza, and as far as Turi, where they carried out a series of raids. There they spent the winter between 73 and 72 B.C. The group split up, and under the leadership of Crixus, the Gauls and Germans reached Mt. Garganus, where they were defeated and killed by the Roman army. Spartacus, however, again took up his project of reaching the north. The Roman soldiers tried unsuccessfully to stop him in Picenum, and in Modena the rebels threw the troops of the proconsul C. Cassius Longinus into confusion. There Spartacus changed his plan, perhaps because he felt that crossing the Alps was impossible. He headed south, once again routing the Roman army in Picenum, and arrived in Calabria, where he reoccupied the city of Turi.

Between the summer and fall of 72 B.C., the Roman Senate entrusted the command of the army to Licinius Crassus, placing him at the head of eight legions (around 40,000 men). This army stationed itself in Picenum. His ambassador, Mummius, was supposed to surround Spartacus and his men, but instead he was taken by surprise and his men were scattered. At this point, Crassus took the lead. He confronted and defeated two detachments of slaves and then began to pursue Spartacus across the Sannius and Lucania. The fugitive unsuccessfully tried to cross the Strait of Messina to take refuge in Sicily. His failure was due, in part, to his betrayal by the Silician pirates. After accepting gifts in exchange for help, they set sail by themselves.

Spartacus tried to avoid direct conflict with the Romans, favoring guerrilla tactics of sudden attack and surprise escape. Once he understood this strategy, Crassus built a fortified wall to shut in the rebels. Fifty-four kilometers long, it ran from the Gulf of Sant'Eufemia to the Gulf of Squillace. In February of 71 B.C., Spartacus—by now short on supplies—managed to scale the wall and continue his flight towards Brindisi. Once more, his heterogeneous group split up, only to suffer two successive defeats in and around a swamp in Lucania; there, the Roman army killed 12,300 rebels, who fought to the death without retreating.

Spartacus again took flight. He encountered and destroyed a Roman detachment. His troops, elated by this victory, made him abandon his evasive guerrilla tactics to confront the Roman troops, just as the latter were swelling with the arrival of the armies of Pompey and Terentius Varro Lucullus. Spartacus's troops and the Roman legions met in a decisive battle near Brindisi, where Spartacus was killed. His death, which became legend, is exalted in the same ancient sources that record his courage and dignity: "he was surrounded by a crowd of enemies and knocked down, all the while defending himself, erect . . . he was wounded on the thigh by a javelin: fallen to his knees, his shield thrown aside, he still resisted his attackers . . . his body was not found" (Appianos *Bellum civile* 1.557–59). In the disappearance of Spartacus's body, mentioned by Appianos, one can almost discern the roots of a popular legend: that Spartacus was not actually dead, but would return once more to lead the oppressed multitudes. Instead, the approximately 6,000 slaves who survived the battle were crucified along the road from Capua to Rome.

The utopia of the slave revolts died out with Spartacus. After his defeat and the extermination of his men, there would be no collective movement for the liberation from slavery for many centuries to come.

This type of building appears to have been invented in Campania. Indeed, the oldest amphitheaters that we know of are in this region, such as the one at Pompeii. Rome was one of the last cities in the Empire to fit up its own amphitheater. Until then, the contests in the capital were held in wooden buildings that were dismantled after each spectacle. The first permanent amphitheater in Rome was built under Augustus, by Caius Statilius Taurus in the Campus Martius (Dio Cassius 51.23.1). After this structure was destroyed in the fire of A.D. 64, Vespasian planned the construction of the Colosseum, which was ultimately inaugurated by Titus in A.D. 80 (FIGURE 24). The site chosen for the Flavian amphitheater was the artificial pool in Nero's *Domus Aurea*; it was a kind of symbolic restitution to the Roman people of the land in the city center, which Nero had appropriated. The colossal bronze statue of Nero (Nero's Colossus), which towered over one side of the amphitheater and probably inspired its name, was preserved but transformed into an Apollo.

Amphitheaters were made up of two essential parts: the *cavea*, where the steps for the spectators were excavated, and the arena, where the games took place. The arena got its name from the sand that covered the ground, allowing the combatants to move around freely. During the Empire, many of the amphitheater arenas rested not on the ground, but on wooden floors that covered a complex system of underground spaces and corridors (*hypogeum*) (FIGURES 24–25). The underground areas were used to keep scenery, props, and caged animals and to provide space for the gladiators' dressing rooms. Occasionally, through a system of winches and elevators, the ornate scenery

FIGURE 25.
Pozzuoli, amphitheater, underground. The spaces with cages for the wild beasts are on the left, on two levels. Above are the openings through which the cages were lifted onto the arena floor.

FIGURE 26.
E. Du Pérac, drawing reconstructing the naval battles of Domitian, 1581.

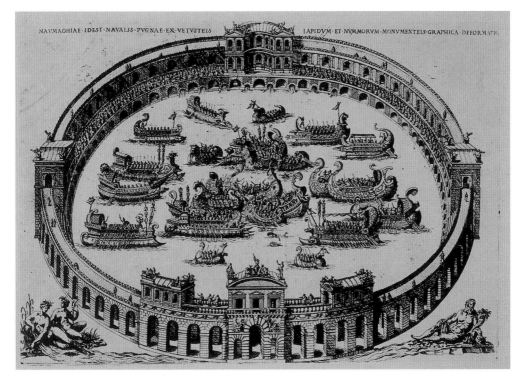

NAVMACHIAE·IDEST·NAVALIS·PVGNAE·EX·VETVSTEIS   LAPIDVM·ET·NVMMORVM·MONVMENTEIS·GRAPHICA·DEFORMATIO

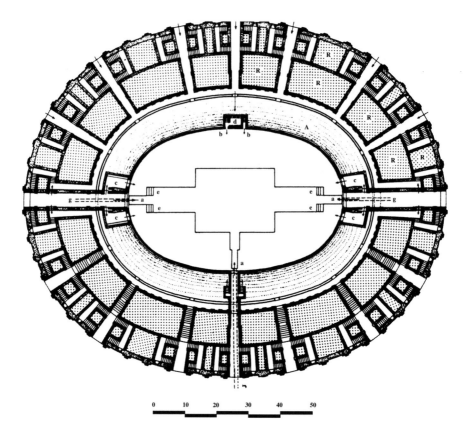

FIGURE 27.
Merida, plan of the
amphitheater with
a basin for aquatic
games.

of the games, the caged animals, and sometimes the gladiators themselves sur-
prised the public by springing directly onto the arena floor.

In those amphitheaters without underground staging areas, such as the
one at Pompeii, all of the technical equipment—the cages and the fighting paraphernalia—was kept in the *carceres*, and possibly in the corridors. To ensure the
safety of the spectators, special precautions were taken, especially during the
shows with wild beasts. Since the most prominent spectators had their seats clos-
est to the arena, and were therefore the most vulnerable, a strong metal net with a
series of elephant tusks protruding from the top was erected between the podium
and the arena. It is widely believed that naval battles (*naumachie*) were also held
in the amphitheaters (FIGURE 26). Some amphitheaters, such as the ones at
Verona and Merida, have been found to have large basins dug into the arena
(FIGURE 27). But it is likely that mostly hippopotamus and crocodile hunts took
place there, as well as the staging of myths involving water (Martial *Liber spectaculorum* 25.25.26). There were probably also aquatic shows with naked dancers—
just as in the theaters—against which Christian authors vociferated. Since they
are too small to allow for the maneuvers of real ships, these basins may have
accommodated small boats or model ships, at the very most.

The big naval battles recalled in classical sources were staged not in the
amphitheaters, but in natural or artificial lakes made especially for this kind

of event (Augustus *Res gestae* 23). The most detailed description we have concerns the big naval show promoted by the emperor Claudius around A.D. 52 on Lake Fucinus, which included triremes, quadriremes, and 19,000 combatants. Among these men, there were not only gladiators and convicts but also soldiers from the imperial fleet (Tacitus *Annales* 12.56; Dio Cassius 60.33; Pliny *Naturalis historia* 3.63; Martial *Liber spectaculorum* 28.11; Suetonius *Claudius* 21). An extraordinary naval show, for which the Circus canals were filled with wine, was produced on the orders of the emperor Elagabalus (Elagabalus *Scriptores historiae Augustae* 23.1).

The *cavea* was divided into three horizontal sections: the *ima*, the *media*, and the *summa cavea* (from bottom to top). Stairways divided the *cavea* vertically, creating wedge-shaped sections of different sizes. These partitions were supposed to create a strict division of places during the spectacles; such divisions were regulated by decree of the decurions. Getting a place with a good view held great importance, and a place of honor in the theaters and amphitheaters was a kind of reward that the city accorded to its most deserving citizens. A good seat not only meant an excellent view of the spectacle, it also allowed one to be seen by others and to show off one's social status (Ovid *Ars amatoria* 1.99; Juvenal *Saturae* 6.352–56).

Thus the division of places in the amphitheaters and theaters reflects the social hierarchy in Roman society. Suetonius recalls that Augustus, impressed by the affront that a senator had faced when he was not able to find a seat in the amphitheater at Pozzuoli, proclaimed a law (*lex Iulia theatralis*) that reserved the first row of seats in the entertainment venues for senators. But the ruling was applied to other social categories as well. He separated the soldiers from the people; he assigned special seats to the married men of the common people, and an individual section to boys under age, and a section adjacent for their tutors. He prohibited the badly dressed from sitting in the middle section. He did not allow women to view even the gladiators except from the upper section, even though it had once been customary for men and women to sit together at the shows (Suetonius *Augustus* 44).

Suetonius's account is confirmed by the archaeological evidence, particularly in inscriptions found engraved on the surfaces of the steps of some of the theaters and amphitheaters of the Empire. These inscriptions reserved places for certain categories of people or certain social groups. In some cases, specific individuals were named. Some places were marked with a simple number on the step, as in the theater at Pompeii or the amphitheater at Verona. In others,

FIGURE 28.
Pozzuoli, amphitheater. Marble fragments indicating the numbered sections CUN (*cuneus*), followed by a number.

33

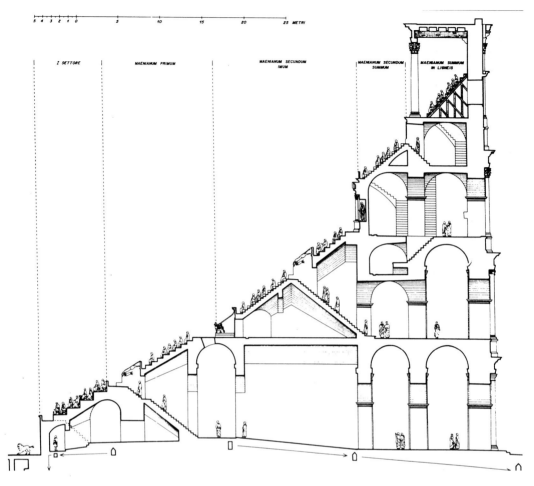

I SETTORE   MAENIANUM PRIMUM   MAENIANUM SECUNDUM IMUM   MAENIANUM SECUNDUM SUMMUM   MAENIANUM SUMMUM IN LIGNEIS

FIGURE 29.
Reconstructed section
of the Colosseum,
showing the division
of places and the corri-
dors leading to them.

like the Colosseum and the amphitheater at Pozzuoli, the arches above the
entrances to various sections of the *cavea* were marked with numbers (FIGURE
28). This numbering system probably corresponded to the number on the
ticket (*tessera*) — usually made of bone — by which spectators located their seats.

The *cavea* was neatly divided into sections, which were officially assigned
to specific categories of spectators, according to their social standing and their
membership in organized groups or corporations. The horizontal divisions produced the clearest demarcation (FIGURE 29): the most important figures were
seated in the *ima cavea*, while the steps behind were open to more modest
spectators. Those without reserved seating hurried to get the best places as early
as the night before, often causing a racket. One night, the emperor Caligula,
awakened by the shouting of the crowds who were trying to find places in the
Circus, ordered his guards to disperse them with clubs (Suetonius *Caligula* 26).

The permanence of the amphitheater made a suitable cover over the *cavea*
indispensable, especially in summertime, and so the velarium was designed.
Although the ancient authors make frequent reference to this amenity, there are
no detailed descriptions of how it worked. Thus archaeologists have expressed

several, not always convincing, hypotheses regarding its mechanics (FIGURE 30). The writer Valerius Maximus (2.4.6) maintains that the velarium was a rural invention, first introduced to Rome by Q. Catulus. Pliny (*Naturalis historia* 36) adds that Publius Lentulus Spinther made technical improvements to it ten years later. The velarium was made with bands of the same very strong linen used in nautical sails. In the Colosseum, the velarium was manipulated by sailors from the naval fleet at Misenum. Their presence was indispensable, not so much for ordinary maneuvers, but in times of bad weather. Their main task was to withdraw the velarium when the winds became too strong. Lucretius (*De rerum natura* 6.108) remarks on the fury of the wind that rocked the velarium, producing thunderous sounds. Martial writes that the velarium remained closed when the wind was too violent (*Epigrams* 11.21.6, 14.28).

The velarium could be decorated—the one in the wooden amphitheater in the Campus Martius simulated a starry vault—or it could be done up in various colors. Lucretius left us a vivid description of the colored velaria:

> . . . *watch the yellow awnings,*
> *The reds, the purples, spread on poles and beams*
> *In some great theatre, where they flutter, billow,*
> *Stir, over the audience, and stain and dye*
> *Not only with actors, but with wavering hues*

FIGURE 30.
Reconstruction of the velarium at Pompeii in a watercolor by P. E. Bonnet, 1859.

FIGURE 31.
Boundary stones
around the outside
perimeter of the
Roman Colosseum
used for anchoring
support cables for the
velarium.

Transform the most distinguished senators
Watching the show; and where the walls are hung
Most thick with color, so much more the day
Indoors appears to smile in all that light
Of lovely radiance. (*De rerum natura* 4.75–83)

This passage by Lucretius also shows that the velarium wasn't stretched taut like the ceiling of a room, but that it adhered rather loosely to the cavity of the *cavea*. This can also be deduced from a passage by Propertius (4.1.15) and from the famous fresco depicting the fight (see page 106) between the Pompeians and the Nucerians (FIGURE 58). At the top of the building there were corbels to support the poles, to which a system of cords and pulleys was attached; these were used to spread out or roll up the velarium. It could be unfolded or taken down very quickly, even while the show was in progress. Suetonius recalls that the emperor Caligula once ordered the velarium to be closed, thereby exposing the detained audience to sunstroke (*Caligula* 26). In Rome, along the perimeter of the Colosseum, one can still see 5 of the 160 boundary stones that served to anchor the cables that supported the velarium (FIGURE 31).

In addition to the velarium, there were other amenities to sweeten a long day in the amphitheater. Much appreciated was the spraying of water, perfumed with crocus or saffron (*sparsiones*), which helped to mitigate the heat and lessen the strong odors produced by the beasts and the enormous crowd (Lucretius *De rerum natura* 2.416; Ovid *Ars amatoria* 1.104; Pliny *Naturalis*

FIGURE 32.
S. Maria Capua
Vetere, amphitheater.
Decorative bust on the
keystone of the arch.

historia 21.33; Martial *Liber spectaculorum* 3.8). According to a description by
Seneca (*Naturales quaestiones* 2.9.2, *Epistulae* 90.15), the water was forced under
pressure through perforated pipes surrounding the outside perimeter of the
arena. It might then rise to great heights before falling in droplets onto the
spectators. There may have been still other mechanisms for producing the
sparsiones. In the theater at Pompeii, one can imagine the presence of reservoirs
on the *summa cavea* from which the water might fall onto the steps, though
not through a jet. Lucan writes about some statues at the top of the *cavea* that
gushed with little springs of saffron water (*Bellum civile* 9.808–10).

The state of ruin in which the majority of the amphitheaters have come
down to us prevents us from fully understanding how rich their ornamentation
could have been. From their remains, it seems that many parts of the
amphitheater were furnished with architectural decorations in marble, or with
paintings, including the screens on the ramps entering the *cavea* (*vomitoria*),
the podium around the arena, and the place of honor for the authorities.
Columns and capitals beautified the main entrances, and there were often
decorative busts over the arches, as in the amphitheater at Capua (FIGURE 32).
Niches and shrines were often resurfaced in marble, while stuccowork and
paintings covered the ceilings and walls of the corridors. In some places, even
the screens placed at the entrances to regulate the flow of spectators were made
of ornate marble. Finally, statues of divinities and munificent civic figures may
have completed the decoration of these entertainment venues.

PART TWO

THE SPECTACLES AT POMPEII

P ompeii is a unique observatory for viewing the life of the gladiators and the organization of the games. Here are preserved not only the amphitheater, the *ludus* where the gladiators trained and probably lived, the armory, and the houses and tombs of the games' organizers but also notices of the spectacles, graffiti drawn by the gladiators themselves, and paintings and objects decorated with gladiatorial scenes, attesting to their popularity.

THE DOCUMENTS:
SPECTACLE PROGRAMS AND GRAFFITI

Without doubt the inscriptions that have made the walls of Pompeii famous are among the most interesting and informative documents we have. Wall writings were plentiful in every populated center of the ancient world, but only in the cities buried by the eruption of A.D. 79 are they preserved in such numbers. To date, more than seven thousand wall inscriptions from Pompeii and the surrounding area have been published. They have been transcribed in Volume 4 of the *Corpus Inscriptionum Latinarum* (*CIL*) and its supplements. The majority of these inscriptions are devoted to Pompeii's final years, but some belong to even more ancient periods.

There are essentially two types of wall inscriptions: those written with a brush, and those etched into the surface. The *edicta munerum*—that is, the programs that announced to the public the shows coming to the amphitheater—were as important as electoral posters, and they were painted by professional scribes (FIGURE 33). Some of these scribes

FIGURE 33.
Wall inscriptions
on the Via
dell'Abbondanza
in Pompeii
(from Spinazzola 1953).
Detail opposite.

D LVCRETI·
SCR CELER
SCR AEMILIVS CELER · SING AD LVNA
SATRÍ·VALENTIS ·FLAMINIS· NERÓNIS· CAESARIS · AVG· FILI·
PERPETVÍ·CLADIATÓRVM·PARIA·XX·ET·D·LVCRETIO·VALENTIS·FÍLI·
GLAD·PARIÁ· X·PVG· POMPEÍS·VI·V·IV· III·PR· ÍDVS· APR·VÉNATIÓ· LEGITIMA·
ET·VELA· ERVNT

FIGURE 34.
Inscription painted in
red in Region IX,
insula 8: "Twenty pairs
of gladiators of
Decimus Lucretius
Satrius Valens, perpet-
ual flamen of Nero
Caesar, son of
Augustus, and ten pairs
of gladiators of his son,
Decimus Lucretius
Valens, will fight at
Pompeii from April
8–12. Fight with wild
beasts according
to normal standards;
velarium will be used."
In the "C": "Celer,
painter." On the side:
"Aemilis Celer painted
this by himself, by
moonlight" (mid-1st
century A.D.).

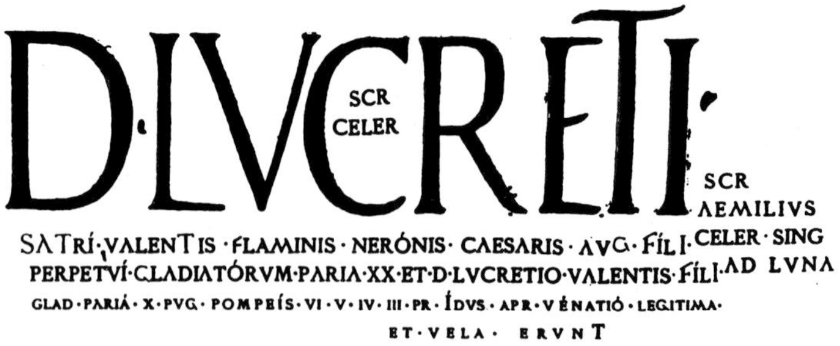

even left their names: one Aemilis Celer boasted that he painted his notice
without any help—there was usually an assistant to hold a lamp—by moonlight ("*Scripsit Aemilis Celer singulus ad lunam*," *CIL* IV.3884; FIGURE 34).

The *edicta* were commissioned by the local magistrates, who were obligated
by law to offer gladiatorial spectacles during their year in office, partly financed
by the city and partly by the magistrates themselves. The wording was almost
identical in each notice, with a few variations or additions. The name of the
editor muneris appeared in the genitive in big letters at the top, followed by the
number of gladiator pairs to be exhibited (*gladiatorum paria*)—usually twenty
paria, or forty gladiators (FIGURE 35). Sometimes notices specifically mentioned the occasion for which the show was being offered (*causa muneris*). In
fact, a magistrate or priest could offer a spectacle for reasons that were not tied
to his municipal and statutory obligations. It might be for the inauguration of
a monument or a public building, as in the case of an altar in Pompeii (*CIL*
IV.1180). Or it might be for the inauguration of paintings (*CIL* IV.1177, 1178,
3883, 7993), or even for a funeral, though this would have been rare during
the Empire. Among the most reported in Pompeii were the *munera pro salute
imperatoris*, spectacles given in honor of the emperor. With these, magistrates
hoped to win the emperor's favor.

The time and place of the performances were almost always announced in
the *edicta*. Thus we know that the majority of the spectacles took place either
on a single day, or over the course of four days. Spectacles lasting two or three
days were not as common. Although there are reports of shows taking place
throughout the year, spring (from March to June) was preferred for the
weather. Sometimes the *edicta* specified that the show would take place only
if weather permitted (*qua dies patientur*), or, contrarily, it would happen "rain
or shine" (*sine ulla dilatione*).

To ensure that the time spent in the amphitheater was comfortable, especially in the summer, a velarium was spread over the top of the building. This
useful amenity was even mentioned in the edicta. There are numerous gladiatorial notices on tombs, especially those outside of the Nucerian Gate (FIGURE
43). This gate adjoined a major road linking the coastal centers (Pozzuoli,
Naples, and Herculaneum) with the south, and the rich, rural inland areas.
Many of the gladiatorial notices refer to the spectacles that were to be given in
these important centers of Campania.

CN·ALLEI·NIGIDI GAVELLVS TIGILLO
ET·CLODIO· SAL
TELEPHI·SVMM· RVDIS
INSTRVMENTVM·MVNERIS
MAI·QVINQ·SINE·IMPENSA·PVBLICA·GLAD·PAR·XX·ET·EORVM·SVPP·PVGN· POMPEIS
V·VA
DIADMENO·ET·PYLADION

Graffiti are inscriptions or drawings that were etched on a hard surface (usually a wall) with a pointed implement (FIGURE 36). Virtually anyone (men, women, and children) who wanted to share their feelings with others— their thoughts, jokes, insults, greetings, or words of love—would write them in this medium. The passion for writing on walls was so widespread that the following couplet, of which three different copies have come down to us, circulated in Pompeii: "It is a wonder, O wall, that you haven't collapsed under the weight of such nonsense" (*CIL* IV.1904, 2461, 2487).

FIGURE 35.
Edictum muneris painted on the facade of the house of A. Trebius Valens (III 2.1): "Twenty pairs of gladiators and their substitutes of the *quinquennalis* Gnaeus Alleius Nigidius Maius will fight at Pompeii. No public monies will be used." On the side, written in smaller letters: "Gavellius hails Tigillus and Clodius; health to you, wherever you go, O, Telephus, *summa rudis* and *instrumentum muneris*," and "Long live Diadumenus and Piladio."

FIGURE 36.
Graffito from a Pompeian wall.

These written documents offer us interesting information on the world of the gladiators. Mostly, they have shed light on the names of the protagonists—the organizers, the agents, the gladiators, and their fans—whose memory would have otherwise completely faded.

THE PLAYERS: *EDITORES*, AGENTS AND *FAMILIAE GLADIATORIAE*, AND GLADIATORS

The *Editores*

The *editores munerum* were responsible for paying all or part of the expenses of the gladiatorial spectacles. Inscriptions in Pompeii testify to the existence of at least nine *editores*, all belonging to the local magistrature.

In the period when Pompeii was a Roman colony, there were two "mayors" at the head of the civic administration, the *duoviri iure dicundo*. They were charged with administering justice and summoning and presiding over the assemblies that elected the magistrates and the city council (*ordo decurionum*). There were also two aediles, who were in charge of street maintenance, public buildings, markets, and public order. Lastly, every five years, *duoviri quinquennales* were elected in place of the *duoviri iure dicundo* for the purpose of updating the census. These officials were in contact with the central government, and they had greater authority than the regular *duoviri*. There were also sacerdotal posts: the pontifex was in charge of the city's official cult, and the augur was an expert in divination. Even the cult of the emperor was administered by a hierarchy of priests and priestesses. The most important were the *flamines Augusti*; members of the lower classes could only become the lower-ranked *Augustales*.

Not only did the city magistrates receive no salary, they were expected to spend large sums of their own money while in office. In fact, they were obligated to offer spectacles or finance public works during that year. Therefore, whoever wanted to undertake a political career needed to be sufficiently wealthy to pay all of the associated expenses. In return, the municipal magistrates enjoyed many honorific privileges.

One Pompeian sponsor was A. Clodius Flaccus; he was *editor* twice, once as *duovir*, and again as *quinquennalis*. He was a member of the local aristocracy under Augustus and belonged to the *gens* of the Clodii, who owned vineyards in the area of Vesuvius and produced the famous wine, *Clodianum*. In a sepulchral inscription, now lost (*CIL* X.1074d), his activities as *editor* were listed in detail.

During his first duovirate (around 20 B.C.), for the feast of Apollo, he orchestrated a solemn procession of all the games' participants through the forum (*pompa*). He presented bulls and toreros, boxers, and three pairs of *pontarii* (a type of gladiator who fought on a platform). He also staged theatrical productions with clowns and mimes, including Pylas, who may have been freed by Augustus and who was famous for creating the pantomime genre.

In his second duovirate (when he was *quinquennalis*), A. Clodius Flaccus offered entertainments to coincide with the *ludi Apollinares*. Again he organized a *pompa* in the forum, and put bulls, toreros, and boxers on display. This time, the theatrical productions were replaced by a day of contests between thirty pairs of wrestlers and forty pairs of gladiators in the amphitheater. Here, it is interesting to note that the epigraphic text divides the number 40 into 35 + 5. This has led some scholars to hypothesize that there were 35 pairs of male gladiators and 5 pairs of female gladiators. As we have noted above, there is some evidence for the presence of women in the arena, but this was still quite an exceptional phenomenon. The participation of women would have been announced beforehand, and this surely would have drawn a very large crowd. There was also a hunt with wild boars and bears, and bullfights. For his third term (3–2 B.C.), only theatrical performances were given, but first-rate actors were used.

Another *editor*, M. Tullius, gave a spectacle in Pompeii from November 4 to 7. From this show we have three *edicta munerum*, written on tombs in the necropolis at the Nucerian Gate (*CIL* IV.9979–81). Tullius, too, was part of a wealthy and powerful family in the Augustan era. He may, in fact, be the same figure who built the Temple of the Fortuna Augusta on his own property, at his own expense. His show included a fight with beasts and twenty pairs of gladiators.

Decimus Lucretius Satrius Valens and his son Decimus Lucretius Valens were two important *editores*. Sometimes, father and son appeared together in the inscriptions as *editores munerum* (*CIL* IV.3884, 7992, 7995, 1185; FIGURE 34). The father held the prestigious appointment of *flamen Neronis Caesaris Augusti fili perpetuus*. But this was not the only tie between him and the emperor. There must have been a close, personal relationship between Nero and Satrius Valens, if we consider the famous painting of the riot in the amphitheater at Pompeii (FIGURE 58). On the walls of the gymnasium, which is also reproduced in the fresco, the following inscription is perfectly legible: "*D. Lucretio fel(l)citer,*" and in Greek letters, "*Satri(o) Oualenti, O(g)ousto Ner(oni) feliciter.*" According to some scholars, this acclamation associating Satrius Valens with Nero suggests that it was actually Satrius Valens who interceded with the emperor so that the amphitheater could be reopened early. The painting would have been commissioned to celebrate this happy occasion.

An inscription etched on a column of the so-called *Campus* of Pompeii casts a questionable light on the wife of D. Lucretius Valens (the son of Satrius) (*CIL* IV.8590). It reports the sale of two top-notch (*primae rationis*) gladiators (an *eques* and a *Thraex-murmillo*) to the wife of Lucretius Valens. However, it is quite strange that a wife should make such a purchase. Furthermore, a magistrate or priest who offered a spectacle wouldn't actually own a *familia gladiatoria* but would only rent the fighters temporarily from an agent. It is therefore likely that the verb "*venio*" has an obscene meaning in this allusion to the wife of the *editor* D. Lucretius Valens. Like many other society matrons, she must have fallen prey to the charms of the gladiators.

Ti. Claudius Verus was another *editor* active during Nero's reign. He offered a spectacle on February 25–26, *pro salute Neronis*, in which there were exhibitions of athletes and hunts — but no gladiators (*CIL* IV.1181, 7989) —

FIGURE 37.
Pompeii, edict
painted on the Via
dell'Abbondanza (III
2.1): "For the inaugu-
ration of the paintings
on wood of Gnaeus
Alleius Nigidius
Maius, on June 13th,
there will be a parade,
a hunt of wild beasts,
fighters, and the
velarium. Greetings
to Nigra (who painted
the notice) Ocella"
(DAIR 61.110).

probably because of the prohibition after the riot of A.D. 59. The term of his duovirate was A.D. 61–62, and on February 5, 62, a terrible earthquake partially destroyed the city. It is indeed curious that, only twenty days after the quake, a spectacle was held. (Granted, it did not take place in the damaged amphitheater, but at another location.)

The aedile A. Suettius Certus was also an *editor muneris* from this period. His spectacle featured the famous *Neroniani* (*CIL* IV.1189–91, 7987).

The final years of Pompeii saw the political activity of still another influential figure, N. Popidius Rufus, who organized a fight with wild beasts. The inscription painted in front of the entrance to the *Ludus Gladiatorius* (*CIL* IV.1186) specifies that the velarium would be rolled out during the show, and possibly—the writing is not altogether clear—apples would be distributed to the spectators. Indeed, some *editores* occasionally gave gifts (*sparsiones*) to the audience.

The most famous organizer of amphitheater shows in Pompeii was Cn. Alleius Nigidius Maius. The inscriptions at Pompeii have given us numerous pieces of information about this figure. He was one of the *duoviri quinquennales* in A.D. 55–56. He held the much sought-after position of flamen, and his spectacles were so lavish that he earned the nickname "prince of the games" ("*princeps munerariorum,*" *CIL* IV.7990). He probably had some part in the riot that broke out in the amphitheater at Pompeii, but he must not have remained involved, since he was still an important figure in the social and political life of the city following that lamentable incident. Some notices (*CIL* IV.1177–78, 7993, 3883) mention spectacles that Maius supposedly gave for the inauguration of an *operis tabularum* (FIGURE 37). Some scholars have linked this event to the inauguration of the new administrative archives (*tabularium*), restored after the earthquake of 62. But others have hypothesized that the spectacles were given for the inauguration of some paintings on wood (*tabulae*) that Maius had commissioned to remind the population of the splendid shows given during his term in office.

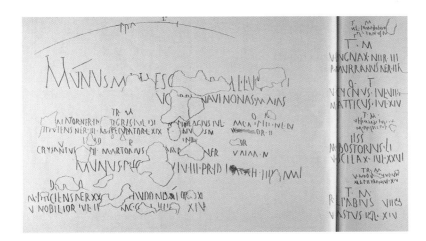

The aedile M. Casellius Marcellus was active in the late Flavian period. He was praised as an able organizer of games in an inscription (*CIL* IV.4999) found near the entrance to what was probably his house (IX 2.26; see "Abbreviations" below for the Pompeian house-numbering system). It is not clear when the *editor* L. Valerius Primus operated; he offered a *munus* as a kind of *augustalis*, or games in honor of Augustus (*CIL* IV.9962).

The Agents and the *familiae gladiatoriae*

The magistrates who were obligated by law to put on *munera* during their year in office retained agents for obtaining the gladiators and organizing the spectacle. A study of the Pompeian *edicta* identifies only three agents, though there must have been others. Actually, it is not always easy to identify the *lanista* in these inscriptions, since the term "*lanista*" is never used, possibly because of the shame that was associated with it.

The most famous agent of Pompeii seems to have been Numerius Festius Ampliatus, who was active between Claudius and Nero. His name appears on two *edicta* and in one inscription painted on a tomb in the necropolis at the Herculaneum Gate, long attributed to A. Umbricius Scaurus (FIGURE 75). Recently, however, the tomb has been attributed to Ampliatus himself. The *edictum* (*CIL* IV.1183) found on the outer wall of the basilica states that the gladiatorial company of Numerius Festinus Ampliatus would give a repeat performance on May 15–16. Evidently, a show that had been given at a prior time had met with such public approval that an encore was requested. The other *edictum* (*CIL* IV.1184), painted on a wall of the *Ludus Gladiatorius*, announced that the *familia gladiatoria* of Festinus Ampliatus would be fighting at Formia. In addition to notifying any Pompeians who would be willing to travel to see their favorite combatants, this inscription probably served as an advertisement for the company, whose fame had reached all the way to that city.

We know of another agent, M. Mesonius, also active during Nero's reign, thanks to a graffito (*CIL* IV.2508) that reproduces the program from a gladiatorial pamphlet (FIGURE 38). The graffito gives the name of the *lanista*, the date

FIGURE 38.
Graffito from Pompeii reproducing a gladiatorial pamphlet (*CIL* IV.2508): "The first gladiatorial spectacle of Marcus Mesonius took place on . . . and May 2nd." The names of the pairs of gladiators and their categories, as well as the outcome of the contests, followed in two columns. Naples, Museo Archeologico Nazionale.

of the spectacle, a list of the pairs of gladiators, and the outcome of the contests. It is interesting to note that in this *munus* there were also famous gladiators from the imperial school: *Iuliani* and *Neroniani*. Their presence attests to Mesonius's ability not only to run his own *familia gladiatoria* but also to obtain other, more prestigious gladiators to improve the quality of his shows.

The *lanista* Pomponius Faustinus is remembered in a graffito placed on a column in the *Ludus gladiatorius*, dating between A.D. 62 and 79. His gladiators signed as a group: *familia gladiatoria Pomponi Faustini* (*CIL* IV.2476). As we have seen, the agent's job was quite burdensome. The large number of gladiators to participate in each fight—usually twenty pairs—required a great deal of effort in recruitment. Furthermore, an agent who desired both fame and money had to obtain good and famous fighters, and this necessitated a superior entrepreneurial sense, as well as an increase in investment.

Agents were always looking out for new talents to replace the gladiators who had been killed or retired. Often they would recruit in the forum, where they could buy slaves or meet adventurous young men or idlers who would do anything to earn money. The agents also had to deal with city authorities to arrange for the use of the amphitheater and to obtain the right to transfer public funds for the spectacles. Finally, they maintained a relationship with the officials of the judiciary and the prison, as they needed access to prisoners who

FIGURE 39.
Reconstruction
of a *venatio* in the
amphitheater at
Pompeii.

had been condemned to death. All of this intense activity must have taken place in some kind of office, and the scholar Rosaria Angelone has hypothesized that one such office was located in Region VII 5.15. Unfortunately, it was completely destroyed by the Anglo-American bombardments of the last war.

The Gladiators

Only rarely do the *edicta munerum* give us the names of the true protagonists of the arena: the gladiators. Precisely because they were meant to give only general information, the notices list the number of gladiatorial pairs to appear without going into detail. Even more limited is the information on the personalities and feelings of the gladiators, which are hardly betrayed by the official notices. However, thanks to numerous rediscovered graffiti, we can deduce important information on the lives, careers, and popularity of the Pompeian gladiators.

The notice of a spectacle put on by the *quinquennalis* Alleius Nigidius Maius names, as one of its attractions, a certain "Ellios" or "Ellius" (*CIL* IV.1179). His name appears at the end of the notice, after announcing thirty pairs of gladiators and a hunt. Apparently, Ellios was so famous that his participation would guarantee a very high turnout and add to the prestige of this particular show. In fact, only when a gladiator or a *venator* had reached the

FIGURE 40.
Quadriporticus of
the theaters used as a
gladiators' barracks
after the earthquake
of A.D. 62.

height of popularity was his name mentioned among the show's attractions. Another *edictus* (*CIL* IV.9975) mentions the famous gladiator Sabinianus, and another graffito reveals that in a forthcoming hunting spectacle, "Felix" would fight against bears (*CIL* IV.1989).

Next to one notice (*CIL* IV.7991), there are words of praise for certain figures who probably circulated in the world of the amphitheater. The most enthusiastic praise is for an ex-gladiator, Telephus, who had earned the wooden sword (*rudis*), symbol of his retirement, and then later was employed as an instructor. He is called "*instrumentum muneris*," or "indispensable tool for the preparation of a show."

Graffiti, more than the official notices, give us a few hints as to the gladiators' personalities. Some were scrawled by the gladiators themselves, and some by their supporters and friends. Most of these graffiti come, naturally enough, from the places where the gladiators lived and trained: the barracks situated in Region V 5.3, which were occupied by gladiators up until Nero's reign, and later, the quadriporticus behind the theater, converted into a barracks after the earthquake of A.D. 62 (FIGURE 40).

On the white stucco of the columns of the barracks portico, many gladiators wrote their names or a few brief thoughts, offering important information about their lives. Thanks to the graffito etched by "Florus," for example, we learn that the gladiators made frequent transfers: Florus writes that he was victorious in Nuceria on July 28, and again on August 15 in the arena of Herculaneum (*CIL* IV.4299). The *murmillo* Samus relates that he lived in that very place (*CIL* IV.4420). Simple signatures to immortalize their names and their roles were left by the *murmillones* Herachinthus and Asicius and the *essedarii* Auriolus, Philippus, and the dreaded Amarantus.

The Thracian Celadus and his friend and rival, the *retiarius* Cresces, left more personal information: they had a common interest in girls. Celadus calls himself the "*suspirium puellarum,*" or "heartthrob of the girls" (*CIL* IV.4342, 4397), as well as the "*puellarum decus,*" or "pride of the girls" (*CIL* IV.4345). In another graffito, the two gladiators appear together: "the Thracian Celadus; Cresces the net-fighter, lord of the girls" ("*Trax Celadus; retiarius Cresces puparru domnus,*" *CIL* IV.4356). In still another graffito, Cresces seems to be vying with his boastful friend, describing himself as "Cresces the net-fighter, doctor to nighttime girls, morning girls, and all the rest" ("*Cresces retiarius puparum nocturnarum mattinarum aliarum ser[.]atinus [..] medicus,*" *CIL* IV.4353).

The gladiators were undoubtedly hugely popular among women. This is confirmed by ancient literary texts, such as the famous passage from the satirist Juvenal cited earlier, and numerous Pompeian graffiti (*CIL* IV.8590). It is the very passion excited by these sweethearts of the arena that led archaeologists to hypothesize about a certain romantic and dramatic love story between a rich matron and a gladiator, after a bejeweled female skeleton was discovered in the Gladiators' Barracks. Perhaps this woman fell victim to the eruption during a daring and fatal encounter with a local champion.

In the same building, there is a heavy-handed joke at the expense of the *murmillo* Lucius Asicius, signed by Jesus, a name that testifies to the presence of Jews in Pompeii. Jesus, playing on Asicius's role as *murmillo*, associates him with a sauce made from cheap fish (*muriola*), and calls him a "little fish," that is, a cowardly and not very manly fighter (*CIL* IV.4287). Numerous other graffiti appear in the quadriporticus of the theaters (VIII 7.16), where the glad-iators were quartered in the city's final years. From here we get the touching testimony of the *provocator* Mansuetus (the name means "tame" or "gentle"), who vows to give his shield to Venus—protectress of Pompeii—if only he might prove victorious (*CIL* IV.283).

FIGURE 41.
Graffito (sketch) of the contest between Severus and the left-handed gladiator Albanus (*CIL* IV.8056).

One drawing (*CIL* IV.8056; FIGURE 41) shows the duel between two gladiators, Severus, the vanquished, and Albanus, the victor. The latter possesses an unusual trait: he is left-handed. In fact, he is not only drawn with his weapon in his left hand, he is also specifically described as *sc(aeva)*, or left-handed, in the writing that accompanies the drawing. Though there are attestations of other left-handed gladiators (*CIL* VI.10180; Seneca *Controversiae* 3.10), a contest with a left-handed combatant apparently merited enough interest to be recorded on the wall. There is even a drawing of a gladiator holding his shield in his right hand and his weapon in his left (FIGURE 42) on one of

FIGURE 42.
Graffito (sketch) depicting the contest between the *Neronianus* Asteropaeus and Oceanus. Pompeii, House of the Labyrinth (VI 11.9)

the columns of the peristyle of the House of the Labyrinth. It is a *Neronianus* named Asteropaeus, victor of Oceanus, who was spared (*m[issus]*) in the end. Left-handed fighters apparently had the advantage during combat, since gladiators were normally trained to fight against right-handed combatants, and an encounter with a "lefty" would upset the ordinary course of a contest.

Numerous notices and graffiti were found on tombs, especially those outside of the Nucerian Gate. On one, a fan made detailed drawings of three memorable moments from a spectacle he attended in the amphitheater at Nola (FIGURE 43). The first scene shows the highly anticipated encounter between the most famous of the *Neroniani (Princeps Neronianus)* and his defeated rival

FIGURE 43.
Graffiti (sketches) from
Tomb 14 EN. Pompeii,
necropolis at the
Nucerian Gate.

Creunus. To emphasize the importance of this encounter, the anonymous artist drew large figures and used a wealth of details, showing even the buglers in the amphitheater.

A second vignette shows the fight between a young gladiator, Marcus Attilius, a free man, against the *Neronianus* Hilarus. It was Attilius's first match, and he was designated a "*tiro*," a title worn by a gladiator at the beginning of his career. Generally, the organizer of a show tried to match two gladiators of equal worth and experience (measured by number of matches fought) (*CIL* IV.1024, 4870). In this case, however, a beginner was pitted against an imperial gladiator who had fourteen fights and twelve victories under his belt. Even so, this newcomer defeated Hilarus, and the upset must have excited the admiration of the Pompeian artist. The last encounter presents, once more, the gladiator Marcus Attilius, matched against a new rival, Recius Felix. Felix, too, was defeated by this boy wonder of the arena.

Those graffiti in which the gladiators' names are accompanied by the outcome of the contest hold special interest: as noted above, the letter "V" means victorious (*vicit*); "M" means *missus*, or defeated but spared; "P" means dead (*perit*) (FIGURES 41–43). These documents have been useful in formulating some statistics that seem to contradict what is generally believed about the outcome of the games. From the accounts of the Pompeian *munera*, it appears that in almost all the contests, the defeated combatant was discharged from the arena alive (*missus est*). On the basis of these data, it has been calculated that, out of a total of thirty-two contests, six gladiators lost their lives, and in one case, a gladiator died after he was spared (*missus obiit*). Apparently, it was in the interest of neither the *editor muneris* nor the *lanista* to let gladiators die, as their training required time and money. Further proof is the number of contests that each individual gladiator had sustained, also minutely recorded in the Pompeian documents. Sometimes the total exceeded seventy.

In some of the graffiti, a child's hand can be recognized. Many boys must have been fascinated by these spectacles and played "gladiators," pretending to be their favorite heroes. In the graffiti with gladiators, particular attention is given to weapons, and this allows us to identify the most common types: *retiarii, essedarii, murmillones, equites, hoplomachi,* and especially Thracians, who were represented most often, and, thus, were the people's favorite. The special admiration inspired by this category of gladiators was also widespread outside of Pompeii, affecting even some of the emperors (Suetonius *Caligula* 54, *Titus* 8). The Thracian's armor was especially elegant, and this must have played a part in winning the public, especially the female public. It was no coincidence that Celadus, the "heartthrob of the girls," was a Thracian. His physical beauty and technical ability made the Thracian a sex symbol. Some vases show Thracians on one side and an erotic scene on the other. On some lamp disks with erotic scenes, the female partner wears the weapons of the Thracian.

THE VENUES

The Amphitheater (II 6)

The amphitheater at Pompeii is one of the most ancient surviving buildings made for spectacles. It was built around 70 B.C. at the expense of the *duoviri quinquennali* C. Quinctius Valgus and Marcus Porcius, two members of Pompeii's wealthy ruling class. Evidence of its antiquity can be seen even in the dedicatory inscription, where the term "*spectacula*" is used, instead of the word for amphitheater, which would not appear until later.

The amphitheater at Pompeii was built in the area to the southeast, partly to take advantage of the embankment that ran along the back of the fortification walls (FIGURE 44). On the north and west sides, however, an artificial embankment was created from the earth cleared out of the arena and the lower part of the *cavea*. From the outside, the lower part presents a series of blind arches. The upper part, too, presents a series of arches, but they are fewer in number and not as high. To reach the upper passageway, two double stairways were built on the west and northwest sides, while two more single stairways were built on both the north and south sides.

The arena (66.80 × 34.50 m) was bordered by a parapet, 2.18 meters high, that was originally adorned with a decoration that will be discussed later (FIGURE 45). It was accessed through two vaulted tunnels (FIGURE 46.1, A

FIGURE 44.
Pompeii, exterior view
of the amphitheater.

FIGURE 45.
Interior view of
the amphitheater
(the arena).

and B), which were paved with basalt blocks to allow the passage of carts that transported equipment necessary for the spectacles. There was a steep descent in each tunnel to compensate for a difference in elevation of almost 4.5 meters between the outer floor and the arena floor.

A third, very narrow, tunnel is found to the west of the short side of the ellipse (FIGURE 46.1, C). This service tunnel connected the arena with the outside. It has been hypothesized that this was the path by which the bodies of gladiators killed in combat were carried out, and that the small space at the end of the corridor (FIGURE 46.1, d) was the *spoliarium*, that is, the place where first aid was given to the wounded, or where slain gladiators were deposited. There is no real evidence for this theory, however. Other scholars have hypothesized, instead, that the magistrates used this corridor, which is also connected to the *ima cavea*, to reach their reserved seats without having to mingle with the crowd. Still another theory holds that the victorious gladiators came up through this passageway to receive their payment.

The amphitheater at Pompeii has no underground chambers, but the four spaces arranged symmetrically at the end of each of the two entrance corridors (FIGURE 46.1, c) were reserved for gladiators and wild beasts. Two smaller passageways on the west side (FIGURE 46.1, H and I) lead to a tunnel, called a "*crypta*" by scholars (f), which runs beneath the lowest seats of the *media cavea* (FIGURE 46.3). This tunnel served both to contain the thrust of the embankment and to allow for orderly seat taking, as the spectators were led to use all of the available entrances and not to crowd toward a single opening. The *crypta* is also accessible through the two main corridors that lead into the arena. All of the passageways and the *crypta* were reinforced with brick arches.

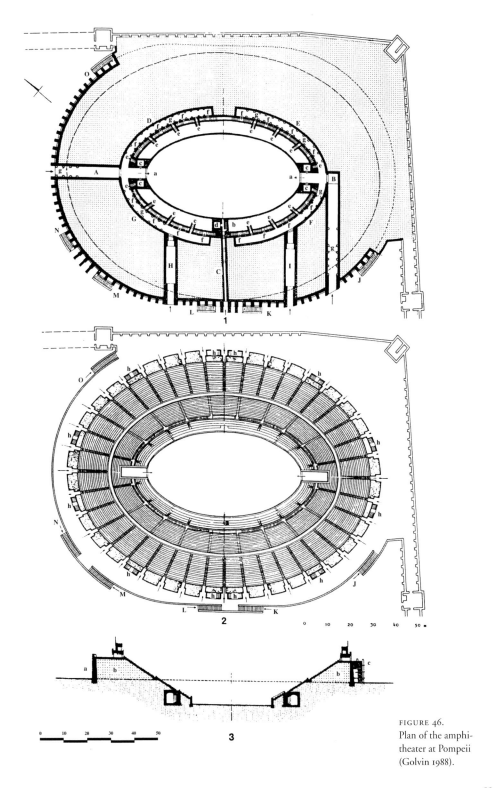

FIGURE 46.
Plan of the amphi-
theater at Pompeii
(Golvin 1988).

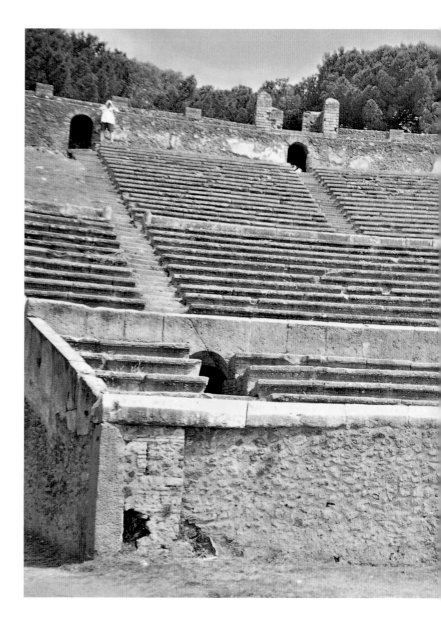

FIGURE 47.
Amphitheater of
Pompeii, interior; detail
of the sections and
their boundaries.

The magistrate Cuspius Pansa and his son undertook this important restoration work after the earthquake of A.D. 62.

The *cavea* is divided horizontally into three parts, which are separated by two balustrades made of tufa blocks (*praecinctiones*) (FIGURE 46.2). In the lowest section (*ima cavea*), there are four large, flat terraces, where the portable wooden seats (*bisellia* or *subsellia*) of the city authorities were placed. The *ima cavea* is separated from the rest of the amphitheater by a continuous balustrade around 80 centimeters high, preventing any exchange between these spectators and the rest of the crowd (FIGURE 47). The middle section (*media cavea*) and

upper section (*summa cavea*), in addition to being divided by a balustrade, are also divided radially (*cunei*) (FIGURES 46.2 and 47), and these wedge-shaped sections are bordered by small steps (*scalaria*) accessible through a series of passages. With the steps laid out in this fashion, the spectators could easily reach their places. The seats were not all made of tufa; where a grassy mantle exists today, they were probably made of wood. And they were not all constructed at the same time, but section by section; rough inscriptions name the magistrates from a neighborhood outside of Pompeii, *Pagus Augustus Felix Suburbanus*, who built the sections of the *cavea* with the money earmarked for games and public illumination.

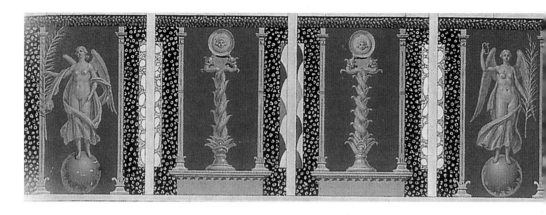

FIGURES 48.
Frescoes from the
amphitheater
(ADS 88).

FIGURE 49.
Frescoes from the
amphitheater
(ADS 79).

The small tufa steps were constructed so that the back was higher than the front, allowing spectators to rest their feet without disturbing the people sitting in front of them. Women sat at the top of the amphitheater, following an order by Augustus that they view the games separately from the men. The amphitheater at Pompeii had a total of twenty thousand places, while the city's population is estimated at around ten thousand. The reality was that many spectators came from nearby cities. This is clear not only from the notices of spectacles in other cities found in Pompeii but also from the famous riot that occurred there. That day's spectacle, offered by L. Regulus, was heavily attended by Nucerians. The podium wall, alluded to above, bore a lively decoration that was still quite visible in 1815, when the excavation of the amphitheater got underway. But within a few months of their discovery, the paintings were already rapidly deteriorating. The unprotected plaster crumbled in the frosts of the early months of 1816. Fortunately, Francesco Morelli had already made some drawings of them, which constitute the only testimony of this important pictorial cycle. The pictures had a specific thematic connection to the monument in which they were housed: next to panels of simulated marble or scales, alternating with candelabra-lit spaces, were painted Victories with palm branches and crowns, and shields of various shapes (FIGURES 48, 50, 51). On the largest panels, there were scenes of animal hunts, and there were also panels with gladiators. One drawing (FIGURE 48) shows two gladiators standing on either side of a small door. Both wear loincloths, hold a sword in one hand and a lance in the other, and wear a *galerus* on their left arm up to their shoulder. The little door was probably not an invention of the artist but a real

RVFVS IIVIR PROLVD I·CAE SE·IVVS·SE·F·CAP·II·II·VIR PRO·LVDLVM·M·CANTRIVS MEM ARC·FILVS IIVIR·PRO·LVD·IV

CVN E·S III F·C·EX·DD

FIGURE 50.
Frescoes from
the amphitheater
(ADS 84).

door, possibly leading to the platform where the seats for the authorities
were located.

Another of Morelli's drawings (FIGURE 49) shows the beginning of a contest. A gladiator with high leggings (*ocreae*) and a white *subligaculum* plays a
horn. The figure beside him is probably a referee, recognizable by his white
tunic and long rod. On the right, another gladiator holds a long rectangular
shield, and still another, partly hidden, holds a feathered helmet in his raised
hand; beside him is an assistant holding a sword. At each end are two Victories
with palm branches and crowns. Two attendants bow before one of them, with
shields and helmets in their hands.

Morelli's drawings also reproduce fights between animals: a bear and a bull
are goaded by being tied together (FIGURE 50) (Seneca *De ira* 3.43.2); a lioness

pursues a horse; a boar is chased by a panther; a lion goes after a deer (FIGURE 51). All the scenes are set in rocky landscapes, which probably allude to the scenography of the amphitheater that was used for such spectacles.

The representation of lions and tigers on the podium of the Pompeian amphitheater is no indication that these animals were actually displayed in the arena. On the contrary, the inscriptions that announced the *munera* never mention such animals. Moreover, the amphitheater at Pompeii doesn't appear to have been endowed with those technical devices that were indispensable to the exhibition of large cats. The safety parapet around the arena, at only 2.18 meters high, was not sufficient to contain the rush of a wild animal, unless nets were added as in other amphitheaters. But in Pompeii there are no traces of such expedients. Therefore, it is likely that in the Pompeian *venationes*, only those animals were displayed that could not leap onto the *cavea* and give rise to unpleasant, and quite unplanned, spectacles.

The illustrations on the podium wall must date to the city's final years. In fact, in the famous fresco that faithfully depicts the amphitheater during the riot between the Pompeians and the Nucerians, the podium decoration is made of simulated marble, in keeping with a practice seen in other amphitheaters (FIGURE 58). Thus, the decoration described above could date to the

FIGURE 51.
Frescoes from
the amphitheater
(ADS 87).

period of rebuilding following the earthquake of A.D. 62 and to the reopening of the amphitheater prior to the ten-year period established at the time of its disqualification.

Naturally, the spectators who sat in the amphitheater from dawn till dusk had a whole set of needs to satisfy, including eating. Since there were no intermissions during the shows, one had to get food either inside the amphitheater, or more likely, in the nearby shops or stalls (FIGURE 52). Beneath the porticoes of the Pompeian amphitheater, itinerant vendors set up their booths, as evidenced by certain, no longer legible, inscriptions. One inscription read that

Cnaeus Aninius Fortunatus had the aediles' permission to occupy a certain space. Sometimes only the hour at which a spot would be occupied was indicated, in order to prevent others from requesting it. Even in the famous fresco depicting the riot of A.D. 59 (FIGURE 58), itinerant vendors of food and drink have set up their tables under the trees. The fact that large plane trees did indeed grow in the square of the amphitheater was confirmed during excavation, when casts of the ancient roots were made.

Spectators of the games also needed public restrooms. No toilets have been found in the amphitheater at Pompeii, but in nearby Palestra—which may

FIGURE 52.
Reconstruction of a day at the Pompeian amphitheater (from Niccolini).

FIGURE 53.
Fresco depicting one of the Fates beside a man in the act of defecating. The inscription above it, *"Cacator cave malum"* sounds like a warning not to use places other than those designated for satisfying certain physiological needs. Naples, Museo Archeologico Nazionale (inv. 112285).

have served as *porticus post scaenam*, given the number of gladiatorial graffiti found there—there was a public latrine that must have served this purpose. There were sure to be some uncouth individuals who sought to relieve themselves someplace closer. In Pompeii, numerous prohibitions are directed at these ill-mannered persons, even in the form of drawings, such as the one from tavern IX 7.22, with the inscription *"Cacator cave malum."* This appears over a depiction of a man in the act of defecating, to warn all those who would decide to satisfy their physiological needs elsewhere than the latrine (FIGURE 53).

Though the *edicta munera* in Pompeii make frequent references to the use of vaporized, perfumed water (*sparsiones*) during the spectacles, no machine or device capable of producing this amenity has been found in the amphitheater. Some scholars believe that the spraying was done by hand, while others have hypothesized, as noted above, that the *sparsiones* were not the expected diffusion of perfumed water, but the distribution of other types of favors such as fruit, coins, etc. The velarium, however, often mentioned in the *edicta munera*, is very visible in the painting depicting the Pompeian amphitheater during the riot of A.D. 59 (FIGURE 58). What is left of the system to anchor the velarium is still preserved at the top of the wall of the back facade. There, one can find the remains of the hollowed stone corbels into which the wooden posts that supported the velarium were driven.

Gladiators' Barracks (V 5.3)

From the early days of the Empire, Pompeii had a *ludus*, a place where gladiators lived and trained. In 1899, a rather unique house was completely exposed in Region V 5.3. Instead of the usual hall, there is a large peristyle surrounded by a portico, around which a number of spaces are arranged (FIGURE 54a). A pluteus decorated with hunting scenes connects the columns of the portico (FIGURE 54b). The house was used as a residence beginning in the first century B.C., as attested by the remains of decorations in the Second Style. Then, between the reigns of Augustus and Claudius, it was converted to receive the *familiae gladiatoriae*. Around one hundred different graffiti made by gladiators were found on the columns of the peristyle. One inscription, in particular, offers some very explicit testimony: "*Samus . . . m(urmillo) idem eq(ues) hic hab(itat)*" (*CIL* IV.4420). It reveals that the gladiator Samus, whose name appears three more times, lived in this house. It is estimated that between fifteen and twenty men, both free men and freedmen, lived with him. The graffiti give us their designations and the weapons they used: *essedarii*, Thracians, *murmillones*, net-fighters, *equites*. Sometimes, the name of their masters (Mesonii, Clodii, Octavii, etc.), their battles, and their victories

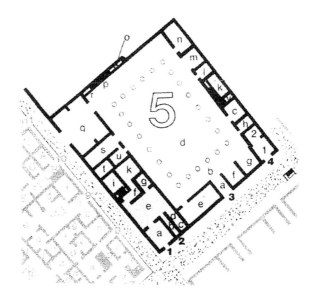

FIGURE 54a.
Plan of the Gladiators' Barracks (V 5.3).

FIGURE 54b.
Gladiators' Barracks (V 5.3). Hunting scenes on the pluteus connecting the columns of the portico.

are also recorded. There are also instances of self-promotion, such as the boasts of the Thracian Celadus and the net-fighter Cresces, mentioned above. The archaeological and paleographic analyses of the graffiti date them between the Augustan era and A.D. 62. The transfer of the gladiators to the largest quadriporticus of the theaters may have been due to damage that their residence sustained during the earthquake of A.D. 62. Also, the ever-growing number of gladiators involved in the games during Nero's reign made a larger building necessary.

Quadriporticus of the Theater (*Ludus gladiatorius*) (VIII 7.16)

The excavation of the quadriporticus in the rear of the theater was carried out between 1766 and 1769 (FIGURE 40). It is a spacious, quadrangular area surrounded by porticoes, built at the end of the second century B.C. (FIGURE 55). Spectators could meet and stroll there during the intermissions, which were often long. The main entrance is near the northeast corner, and it could be reached by passing through the corridor between the theater and the Odeion. The quadriporticus could even be visited on days when there were no shows, by using a passageway (FIGURE 55, 2) connecting directly to the Via Stabiana.

On the northwest side, a stairway connects the quadriporticus with the area of the Doric Temple. After the earthquake of 62, this building was converted into the gladiatorial *ludus*. The gladiators' quarters were narrow spaces (around 10–15 sq m), laid out on two levels with a wooden gallery, each accommodating two or three men. The rooms did not communicate with one another, and apparently there were no beds; the gladiators probably slept on straw mattresses.

There were common rooms—the kitchen (FIGURE 55, 12), the adjoining storehouses (10–11), and a dining room (16)—but there was no second story. On this same side, a prison was discovered. Given the position of the iron shackles, it is clear that the prisoners were not able to stand, but only to bend over, or lie down. The skeletons of four unfettered men were found in the prison.

An apartment, probably for the instructor, was found on the second floor of the east side, near the dining room and kitchen. Space 18, beside the stairs leading to the triangular forum, had been turned into a stable, and the skeletons of both a horse and a man, possibly a stableboy, were found there. In the middle of the south side is an exedra (9), decorated with frescoes in the Fourth Style. In the back of the room Mars and Venus are depicted, and on the sides there are representations of trophies with gladiatorial arms (FIGURE 55). The open area in the middle was apparently reserved for the gladiators' exercises (FIGURES 40, 55). A sundial was also found, perhaps used to establish the time for the training sessions.

In the *ludus*, some magnificent gladiatorial weaponry was found (around fifteen helmets and shin guards, the remains of some ornate metal belts, three caps for net-fighters, one shield, some daggers, and a lance), as well as the remains of two wooden chests containing pieces of cloth for the gold-embroidered costumes, probably worn by the gladiators during the parade. Some helmets (inv. 5638, 5640, 5650, 5657, 5674) and leggings (inv. 5664–8, 5675) bear the stamped initials "PMC" or "MCP"; one *ocrea* bears the monogram "NER.AUG" (inv. 5648), and another "NER" and "MCP" (inv. 5665). According to some scholars,

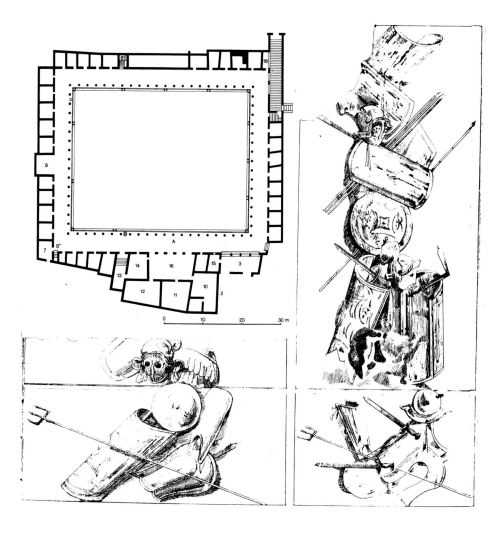

FIGURE 55.
Pompeii, plan of
the quadriporticus
of the theaters, and
a reproduction of
frescoes with trophies
and gladiatorial arms.

these initials belonged to the agents who rented out their weapons along with their fighters, but they could also belong to the weaponsmith; "NER AUG" or "NER" show that the weapons belonged to the *Neroniani*.

The presence of weaponry in the *ludus* suggests that there was no fear of a Spartacus-like insurrection. Furthermore, the gladiators were free to come and go from the barracks and to receive guests there, as demonstrated by the discovery of a bejeweled female skeleton in one of the cells. The discovery of a newborn's skeleton suggests that some gladiators lived in the *ludus* together with their families.

Schola armaturarum (III 3.6)

This important public building opens with a large entryway onto the Via dell'Abbondanza. It was built after the earthquake of A.D. 62, on the site of a previous dwelling, of which some traces remain on the north side. The building was considered a kind of boarding school for the *Juventus pompeiana*

(Pompeian youth), but more recently it has been hypothesized that it was a depository of gladiatorial armor. Two trophies are painted on the facade of the two columns flanking the entrance (FIGURE 56): the one on the left shows a pile of arms at the foot of, or hung to, a tree trunk. At the bottom is a tunic embroidered with tritons and winged griffins. There is a helmet at the top, and pairs of lances are at the sides. On either side of the tunic is a series of shields, and on the left is a heavy anchor, possibly an allusion to naval victories. Part of another red tunic is visible above. At the bottom of the right column, a cart is partly covered by a white bearskin. Around the cart, there is a series of shields and lances; to the right, a large horn. Part of a tunic attached to a tree trunk is just barely visible above.

These decorations, which were widespread in the Roman world, were meant to commemorate naval and land battles. The trophies depicted at Pompeii were copies of large trophies erected in Rome to commemorate the victories of Caesar and Augustus. The large room at the back (8.5 × 8.5 m) was articulated with columns supporting cabinets; the rough wall reveals many holes that were used to anchor the wooden cabinets. Their golden decorations, together with the yellow architectonic lines of the ornamentation below, must have been magnificent. The cabinets probably held weaponry, but only the handle of an ivory sword, representing the head of Minerva, was found.

Beneath the cabinets, the wall is frescoed with red panels, showing winged Victories at the center. These very figures have led scholars to link this building with the gladiators. The ten Victories bear typically gladiatorial weapons and shields, such as curved daggers, or the small round shield of the Thracians.

FIGURE 56.
Pompeii, *Schola
armaturarum* (from
Spinazzola 1953).

REPRESENTATIONS OF GLADIATORS:
PAINTINGS AND RELIEFS

Aside from the existence of numerous graffiti, the popularity of the gladiators at Pompeii is also witnessed in painting, but unfortunately almost all of these representations have been lost. Traditionally, these depictions are numbered in the so-called popular or plebeian genre, which included scenes of everyday life, erotic paintings, insignia from shops picturing the arts and trades, and religious processions and ceremonies.

Going beyond the limited sphere of funerals, the gladiatorial paintings began to appear in domestic and civil decor during the second century B.C. According to Pliny the Elder (*Naturalis historia* 35.52), the first person to commission paintings of gladiatorial contests was C. Terentius Lucanus, who in the second century B.C. displayed paintings done to commemorate the *ludus* he had sponsored in the Grove of Diana at Nemi. Following Augustus's reform of the *munera* (Suetonius *Augustus* 45), the iconography of the gladiators tended to become more exact, and certain schemata were established that were designed to please. The weapons and armor that characterize the different types of gladiators were delineated with more precision, and a great deal of emphasis was placed on these details in the representations.

Paintings of the gladiators became widespread during Nero's reign (A.D. 54–68), as witnessed by both the Pompeian paintings and the literary sources. Pliny the Elder writes that one of Nero's freed slaves had the porticoes of the city of Anzio decorated with portraits of all the gladiators and assistants involved in the *munus* he sponsored (*Naturalis historia* 35.52). This information occasions some significant reflection: first, since the paintings were done prior to the contests—they included all of the participants in the *munus*—their aim was not to commemorate, but to decorate; second, they were done on canvas—a background that had never before been used in Italy—proving that a sense of artistic ambition could be found even in gladiatorial portraiture. Finally, it is significant that these portraits were displayed in public. An epigraph from Benevento (*CIL* IX.1666) mentions the practice of decorating porticoes and basilicas with gladiatorial paintings.

An analogous situation has also been hypothesized for Pompeii. According to Sabbatini Tumolesi, a notice of the *munera* offered by Alleius Nigidius Maius with the formula "*dedicatione operis tabularum*" (*CIL* IV.1177–78, 3883, 7993) refers to spectacles that were offered for the public inauguration of a number of paintings on wood, whose subject was the games that Maius had offered when he was *quinquennalis* (FIGURE 37). Perhaps these commemorative pieces were done in the postriot period, when gladiatorial fights could no longer take place in the amphitheater, and only athletic spectacles and hunts (*venationes*) were allowed. With these paintings, therefore, Maius must have wanted to awaken in the citizens of Pompeii the memory of the splendid shows he had offered in A.D. 55, and with it, a wish for the restoration of those games, so adored by the population. The creators of the painted advertisements that publicized forthcoming shows must have been inspired by these and other depictions of the *munera*. Even though their representations were rough and hurried, and simply executed with ochre or charcoal, they attracted a great deal of interest, as the poet Horace relates (*Saturae* 2.7.96).

As for the diffusion of painting on a gladiatorial theme in the domestic sphere, important evidence is offered by a passage in Petronius's *Satyricon* (29.9). In Trimalchio's house, the painting of a contest given by a certain Laenas was prominently displayed on the wall of the peristyle. Beside it were scenes from the *Iliad* and the *Odyssey*. Such a juxtaposition of literary subjects with games has been seen as a sign of bad taste and ignorance on the part of this parvenu. We don't know Laenas's identity, but what is striking is that, in commissioning the painting of a *munus* offered by someone else—thus, without any intent to commemorate or portray himself—Trimalchio is merely expressing his pleasure at being able to look upon his favorite spectacle.

Finally, the *Satyricon* also illustrates the practice of decorating graves with scenes from the *munera* (71.6). These representations were not meant to illustrate the *munera* organized on the occasion of private funerals, but rather to record the games that notable figures had offered to the citizens.

In Pompeii, we find gladiatorial paintings in private houses, public buildings, and funerary monuments, as witnessed by the literary sources. There were essentially two methods of representing the *munera*—the painting or the frieze. Friezes, often laid out one above the other, were well-suited to extended surfaces, because a combat motif could be repeated over and over again, according to the wall to be decorated. A painting, on the other hand, was more appropriate for rooms or household shrines. Usually, the pictures show the beginning of a contest, or its conclusion, when the defeated gladiator asks for the *missio* and the victor hovers over him threateningly. The depictions of *munera gladiatoria* might generically represent this much-loved spectacle, or they might refer to a specific event. In the latter case, the names of the combatants and the outcome of the contest were reported, witnessing not only the admiration inspired by these divas of the day but also the need to historicize the event, fixing it in the collective memory.

In Pompeii, there are numerous frescoes of fights between animals, often set in mountainous landscapes (FIGURE 57). These representations probably reminded the Pompeians of the *venationes*, which often used scenery with rocks, hills, and waterways. This kind of set was adopted to represent certain myths that included animals. Thus, even the wild beasts of the amphitheater were expected to play a specific role in the staging of a myth. Among the legends that were represented, a special place was held by the myth of Orpheus, who tamed wild beasts with his music and song. Varro reports that one such spectacle was given to entertain the guests at a dinner party in the villa of Quintus Ortensius (*De re rustica* 3.13).

1. Paintings of Gladiators in Homes and Public Buildings

HOUSE OF ANICETUS (I 3.23)   The famous fresco of the riot that broke out in the amphitheater of Pompeii in A.D. 59 between the Pompeians and the Nucerians (FIGURE 58) was discovered on the west wall of the peristyle (FIGURE 59, n) of this house (Tacitus *Annales* 14.17). The painting was flanked by two smaller paintings of gladiatorial pairs, but these were left in place and they soon deteriorated. Moreover, the painting of the riot covered another older painting, also on a gladiatorial theme. It was seen and described at the time of the excavation, but was not otherwise documented. It represented a trophy table with palm branches and incomplete renderings of athletes, whose names were written in Greek characters above ("*Sokrion . . . perdis Teimeas, Apate*"). The owner of the house must have been connected to the concerns of the amphitheater in some way, since the wall of his peristyle was painted with gladiatorial scenes. The second time, he even ventured to choose the very bloody episode of the riot of A.D. 59. On the basis of an inscription

FIGURE 57.
Painting showing a struggle between animals (wolves, boars, stags, lions, rams, and bulls). Pompeii, House of the Ceii (I 6.15).

71

FIGURE 58.
Fresco depicting
the riot between
Pompeians and
Nucerians from the
House of Anicetus
(I 3.23). Naples, Museo
Archeologico Nazionale
(inv. 112222).

painted next to the entrance ("*Anice(te) fac,*" *CIL* IV.2993), and on a series of other acclamations in which Anicetus is billed as "master of scenes" (*CIL* IV.5399, 3877), Della Corte has hypothesized that a famous gladiator, subsequently freed, lived in this house.

Because of its historical content, the painting of the riot, now at the Museo Archeologico Nazionale in Naples (inv. 112222), holds great interest. The artist chose a vantage point from above, with the arena facing the viewer; only part of the velarium is shown, allowing for a look at the activities inside. Even with its errors in perspective, the fresco is exceptionally faithful regarding the representation of the different areas: the amphitheater with its characteristic double stairway leading to the *summa cavea*, the walls with their towers, the gymnasium with its pool in the center, and even the plane trees in the open space—all of this provides us with a "snapshot" of the period.

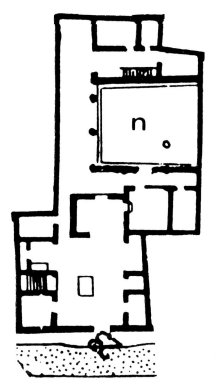

FIGURE 59. Plan of the House of Anicetus (I 3.23).

As for the two small paintings with pairs of gladiators, Sogliano and Fiorelli give almost identical descriptions. For the first painting: "A pair of gladiators in which the victor pursues the vanquished; fallen to his knees, the latter awaits his death before his opponent." For the second painting: "Similar pair, but the vanquished has fallen flat on his face, and behind the victor is a woman who seems to want to speak with him." These descriptions of the small paintings perfectly match the two drawings reproduced here (FIGURE 60). Scholars such as Reinach consider them generically Pompeian (*Répertoire des peintures*, 285, 5).

TAVERN (I 4.27) The only evidence of the painting with gladiators that decorated this tavern comes from Sogliano's description: "Pair of gladiators in combat; they are armed with crested helmets, large, rectangular shields, leggings, and swords." No trace of the fresco remains today.

HOUSE OF THE SACERDOS AMANDUS (I 7.7) After the most recent crumbling of plaster, a fresco with gladiatorial combat in the Second Style was brought to light on the right wall of the vestibule of this house (FIGURE 61, a). It constitutes the oldest evidence of the existence of this pictorial genre at

a

FIGURES 60a–b.
Scenes of gladiatorial
combat (from
Schreiber, pl. 28).

b

Pompeii (FIGURES 61–62). The painting is a kind of frieze, 2.06 meters long, 45 centimeters high, standing 1.60 meters above the ground. The figures were traced on rough plaster using a technique in red monochrome. On the far right is a grotesque figure with the head of an animal, playing a long trumpet. Two fighters on horseback follow, both armed with round shields; one pursues the other, wounding him with a long lance. Above the attacker is an inscription in the Oscan language that reads, "*Phili[......] ans.*" Above the wounded horseman, a very legible inscription reads, "*Spartaks.*" On the left, a duel between two dismounted gladiators (Samnites?), armed with swords and rectangular shields, is pictured. Some undecipherable traces of Oscan letters can be seen above their heads. The painting ends with some kind of a construction (an altar?), no more identifiable than the letters themselves.

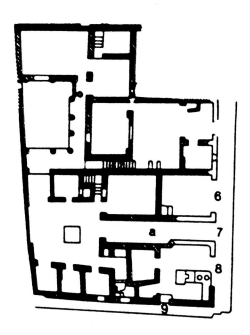

FIGURE 61.
Plan of the House of the Sacerdos Amandus.

FIGURE 62.
Gladiatorial painting, House of the Sacerdos Amandus.

The name of Spartacus immediately generated a lot of interest in this fresco. Maiuri believed the painting had been done after the death of this hero of the slave revolt, who had certainly exercised a great deal of influence in the Vesuvian region, where his first battles were staged. Other scholars went even further: the German archaeologist K. Lehmann-Hartleben proposed a theory that was rather sensational, but turned out to enjoy wide

FIGURE 63.
Exterior of the House
of Loreius Tiburtinus.
Frescoes in their cur-
rent condition.

FIGURE 64.
Drawing by Morelli,
possibly from the
Tavern VII 4.26
(ADS 574).

acceptance. He maintained that the fresco represented the death of Spartacus exactly as it happened. The killer was supposedly a Pompeian man named Felix (the integration of the Oscan name "*Phili[ks pumpaii]ans*" visible over the attacker). He also suggested that the house in which the painting was found belonged to Felix himself. This theory may find confirmation in an account by Appianos (*Bellum civile* 1.120.557), according to which Spartacus was wounded on the thigh during his last battle, just as this painting depicts.

Recently, another theory has been proposed; though less suggestive, it is perhaps more reliable. According to this theory, the painting supposedly antedates the revolt of Spartacus (73–71 B.C.), and is even prior to 89 B.C., when the process of Pompeii's Romanization, including the progressive replacement of Oscan language and culture, began. It alludes to a gladiatorial spectacle, as revealed by the masked *tibicen* or horn player. Therefore, the name Spartacus is not a reference to the commander of the revolt. Spartacus was a very common name in Thrace, and perhaps the gladiator shown here was a Thracian who had earned a certain degree of fame by fighting at Pompeii.

House of D. Octavius Quartius, alias Loreius Tiburtinus (II 2.2–5)   A frieze, eight centimeters high, painted roughly with gladiatorial scenes and contests, was discovered on the back facade of this house, on the side towards the amphitheater, but today these scenes are completely lost to us (FIGURE 63). The original length of the frieze has been estimated at 16.5 meters, but at the time of excavation, the surviving piece measured only 7.3 meters. On either side of the painting was an electoral program. According to Maiuri, these representations may indicate that the proprietor of this wealthy residence was an *editor munerum*.

Tavern (VII 4.26)   Fiorelli reports that a painting with the "scene of a gladiatorial contest and some animals engaged in a struggle" was discovered in the cubicle of this tavern. Some have attempted to identify this now-lost fresco with a drawing by Morelli (ADS 574; FIGURE 64). But such an identification belies the caption accompanying the drawing, which places the painting "in a hall not far from the west gate of Pompeii." However, the same drawing has been considered a copy of some frescoes either from the building VII 5.14–15 or from the *Insula occidentalis*, or even from the amphitheater itself. The confusion probably stems from the fact that the painting was copied several times; to wit, the fresco located outside the Tavern of Purpurius (FIGURE 69) reveals a very similar composition. And so it is likely that a painting similar to the one reproduced in Morelli's drawing, which reflected rather widespread criteria of composition at Pompeii, was frescoed in this tavern.

Alla Porta Settentrionale di Pompei

FIGURE 65a.
Glass vase found in
Hungary. At the bot-
tom, four gladiators in
pairs, with their names
written above. One of
the pairs is Petraites
and Prudes.

FIGURE 65b.
Schematic of the
vase's figures.

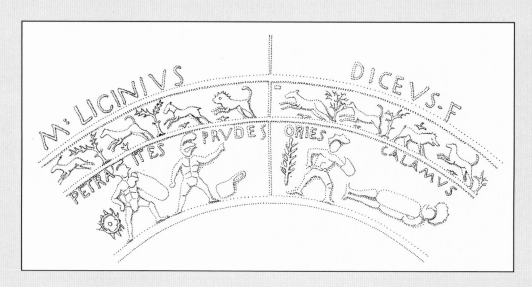

VII 5.14–15   A painting with gladiatorial scenes was discovered on April 12, 1817, on the column at the side of the entrance to this building. Exposed to the atmosphere, it gradually deteriorated. Today, not even the building in which it was housed exists, as it was destroyed by American bombardments during World War II; in its place stands a café-restaurant.

But we do have several descriptions of it. Two gladiators in two different phases of combat were pictured: the beginning of the contest in the upper background, and its conclusion in the foreground below; here, one gladiator was on the ground, and the other was about to land a mortal blow. The fish portrayed on their helmets showed that both gladiators were *murmillones*. Above their heads were the names Tetraites and Prudes and a list of the fights they had sustained. These two gladiators were very famous, and their names appear on glass vessels found in France, England, and Hungary (FIGURE 65). In all of these depictions, Tetraites (sometimes written as "Petraites") is the victor, and Prudes is the vanquished. The name Petraites even occurs in two different places in Petronius's *Satyricon*: once, Trimalchio boasts about his silver cups decorated with the fights of Hermeros and Petraites (52.3); later, he advises his friend, the *marmorarius* (marble worker) Habinnas, to decorate his own grave with depictions of all the contests of Petraites (71.6).

Given the subject matter treated here, Fiorelli believes the building was the workshop of a weaponsmith. Recently, however, Rosaria Angelone has hypothesized that it was the agency of a *lanista*, the owner and instructor of slaves destined to become gladiators. In this "office" in the forum, he would have organized the spectacles that were so well loved by the Pompeians. According to Angelone, the agent was able to bring these two famous glad-iators to Pompeii to fight their tenth (for Petraites) and eighteenth (for Prudes) matches. But the fresco could also simply represent two of the crowd's favorites. Still, other famous gladiators have been immortalized in Pompeii, such as Spiculus, Nero's personal favorite (Suetonius *Nero* 30.2, 47.3), who was depicted in the entrance to the House of the Faun (*CIL* IV.1474).

HOUSE OF C. HOLCONIUS RUFUS (VIII 4.4)   A systematic excavation of this house was begun in 1860 and concluded a few months later (FIGURE 66). On the left column of the entrance hall (12), the painting of a gladiator labeled "*PRIMIgenius*" was uncovered.

No trace of this image exists today. From the accounts of Minervini and Fiorelli, we can gather that the figure of the gladiator was drawn in red on the bottom half of the wall. The fighter was armed with a helmet, a sword, and a rectangular shield. In the same space were depictions of animals taking flight.

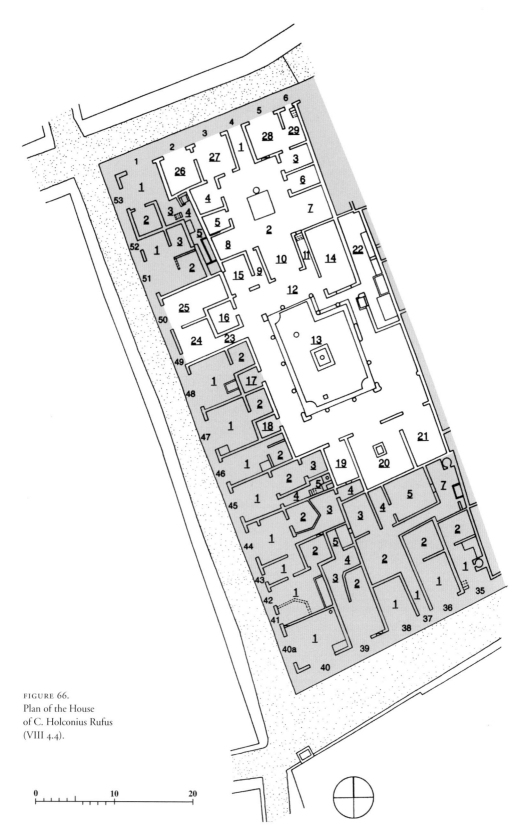

FIGURE 66.
Plan of the House
of C. Holconius Rufus
(VIII 4.4).

0   10   20

FIGURE 67.
House of the Red
Walls, shrine with
gladiatorial arms
(DAIR 71.11).

HOUSE OF THE RED WALLS (VIII 5.37)   In the atrium of this house,
which was being renovated in A.D. 79, there is an aedicula-type shrine on a
high podium (FIGURE 67). Its columns are painted to look like marble. On the
back wall, flanked by *lares*, there is a household Genius with veiled head and a
cornucopia, in the act of making a sacrifice. The tympanum of the aedicula
was decorated with a representation of gladiatorial weaponry, now completely
lost. In the center there was a helmet; on the left, leggings; and on the right, a
shield and a sword.

HOUSE OF THE SCULPTOR (VIII 7.24)   In the peristyle on the south
section of the east wall (FIGURE 68, 12), next to the scene of a naval battle,
there was a painting in the Second Style that depicted the encounter between
two gladiators armed with swords and rectangular shields. The gladiator on

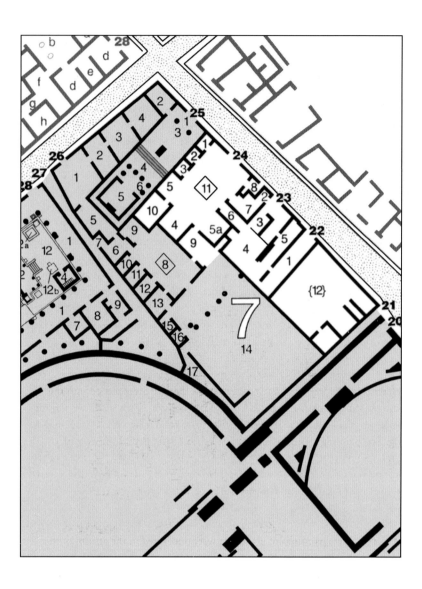

FIGURE 68.
Plan of the House
of the Sculptor.

the right appeared to be off balance, either because he had received a mortal blow or because he was himself attempting to deliver one. Some very decayed scenes of *venatio* followed. One part of the fresco was detached and moved to house I 8.17; another part was left in place, and it has almost completely faded away.

IX 3.13   This painting, too, has disappeared. It is known to us only through the concise descriptions made by Fiorelli and Sogliano. In particular, Fiorelli tells us that in the first room of this shop, beneath the small stairway that led to the mezzanine, a shrine with a Genius flanked by *lares*, the caricature of a male head, and two gladiators in combat were painted. Sogliano reports that the painting was done in red monochrome on white plaster.

TAVERN (IX 9.8)   In 1887, two different layers of plaster were uncovered on the left wall of the first room of this tavern. On the older of the two, which had been scraped to add the second layer, there was a painting of gladiatorial combat. It survives only in the descriptions of Sogliano and Mau, who were not in complete agreement. The part of the fresco that was preserved (60 cm high, 50 cm long) showed a gladiator (a *murmillo*?) turned to the left, with a large, curved, rectangular shield; he was protected by a legging on his left leg and a crested helmet with perforated visor. He wore a cuirass and a *subligaculum*, held a sword, and probably wore a sleeve on his right arm. A black bandage was wrapped around his right thigh, above the knee. His left leg was stretched out in front, his shield was lowered almost to the ground, and his head was turned, as if awaiting the decision on his defeated opponent; the opponent, however, was nowhere in sight. Above this figure, the following text was found: . . . AEDIM SULL XIIX V (*CIL* IV(SUPPL.).3789). According to Sogliano, "AEDIM" was what remained of the gladiator's name. His armor indicates that he was a Samnite. "XIIX" was the number of contests he had fought, and the letter "V" meant that he was victorious in this particular contest. But the most precious element, for Sogliano, was the indication of the gladiatorial *familia* to which he belonged: the *familia Sullana*. Since the *thermopolium* (bar for hot and cold drinks) was located almost in front of the Gladiators' Barracks (V 5.3), and the gladiators were avid about exercise, the reference to the *familia Sullana* suggests that the gladiators moved into the barracks during the Sullan period. Yet the description of the gladiator and his paraphernalia—in particular, his helmet—makes this hypothesis unconvincing. The painting seems to belong, instead, to a later period (first century A.D.). Its proximity to the *ludus* suggests that this was the meeting place of the gladiators quartered there. It may be that, when the gladiators were transferred to the quadriporticus of the theaters after the earthquake of A.D. 62, the place was redecorated to better suit the new clientele.

IX 9.D   Two paintings of gladiators were uncovered in the atrium of this house when it was discovered in 1889. The first one was on the wall to the right of the entrance, and it was already quite damaged at the time of its discovery. A gladiator turns towards the right, painted in red on a white background. His left leg is extended in front of him, in keeping with a compositional scheme that was fairly common to this genre. Mau described it in this way: "The left leg is placed in front; the left foot is higher than the right, and the leg is protected by a large legging that goes up over the knee, to which a cord is attached. The left hand (or so it appears), its arm wrapped, is stretched back beside the thigh, and holds a pole horizontally: the long red line is visible at .85 meters." The other fresco was found in the space adjoining the entrance. Also in poor condition, it depicts two gladiators, each with a large yellow shield and a gilded helmet. The gladiator on the right wears a legging on his left leg and a bandage around his right knee. His opponent wears high

leggings on both legs. This may have been a typical encounter between a *murmillo* and a *hoplomachus* (or a Thracian).

TAVERN OF PURPURIUS (IX 12.7)   The facade of house IX 12.7, located at the corner of a crossroads, was brought to light in 1912. As was often the case with houses near intersections, its facade was decorated with a shrine dedicated to the gods of the crossroads (FIGURE 69). A Genius making a sacrifice between two *lares* is depicted on top. Next to this painting is a monochrome painting (75 × 54 cm) representing the final encounter between two gladiators, both of whom are armed with curved rectangular shields, helmets, and armbands (FIGURE 70). One wears high boots, the other a legging and a knee guard. The gladiator on the right has a bloody wound on his knee. Exhausted from combat, he is on the verge of collapse. The victor, probably a *Thraex*, is using his shield to ward off his opponent's last, feeble blow.

Beneath these paintings are depictions of two serpents (*Agathos Daimon*), and beside them, five priests (*Magistri vici*) in the act of making a sacrifice. This painting covered an earlier one on the same subject. Perhaps it was meant to conceal the Genius of Augustus/Nero, affected posthumously by the *damnatio memoriae*, which dictated that the emperor's name and image be wiped out wherever they appeared. According to Vittorio Spinazzola, who discovered it, this painting was connected to the activities of the house's occupant. Its presence in a household shrine can be considered a request for the protection of the gods of the crossroads.

THE SUBURBAN BATHS

In December of 1985, during the excavation of the Suburban Baths at Pompeii, various fragments of plasters painted with gladiatorial scenes belonging to the Fourth Style were discovered on the upper south wall of the entrance corridor (FIGURE 71, B). They remain at the site today. The paintings exist on two registers, one above the other: a predella (45 cm high, 2.26 m above the ground) and a higher

FIGURE 69, OPPOSITE
Tavern of Purpurius,
Pompeii (from
Spinazzola 1953).

FIGURE 70.
Tavern of Purpurius.
Detail of the painting
with gladiators (from
Spinazzola, 1953).

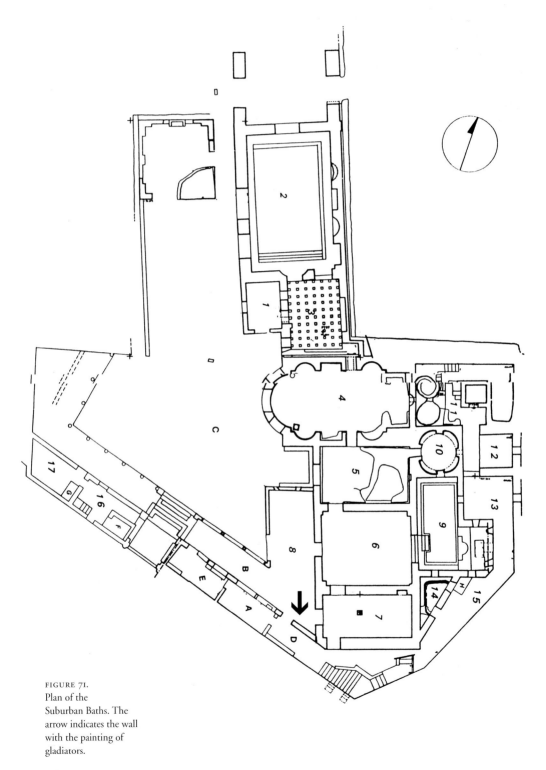

FIGURE 71.
Plan of the
Suburban Baths. The
arrow indicates the wall
with the painting of
gladiators.

area, of which 95 centimeters is preserved lengthwise. Today, only part of the predella and the higher part of the side located to the east of the door between corridor B and room D are preserved. But when the discovery was made, some fragments of the predella on the column to the west of the door were also uncovered; they had broken off due to extreme deterioration.

The first figure on the left of the predella—the one remaining at the site—is a gladiator turned towards the left, who seems to be holding a round shield, of which the lower edge is barely visible (FIGURE 72); everything from his waist up is missing. The second gladiator is also turned towards the left, and he holds a small circular yellow shield, visible only at the lower edge. Though the third gladiator's upper body is also full of lacunae, he is the best preserved, and from this one numerous details can be gathered. The figure is advancing towards the right, his left leg is bent in front of him, and the other leg is stretched straight behind. He wears a white *subligaculum*, with a red *balteus*

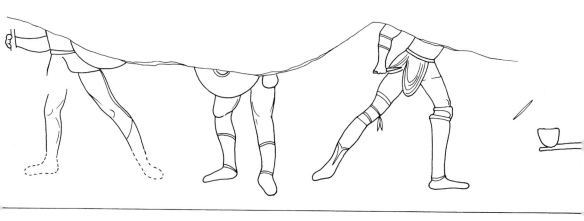

tied around his waist. On his left leg is a knee-high *ocrea*. His right leg is protected by a high green band at the knee, tightened with red laces; he wears a special little legging around his right ankle, which almost reaches his calf. This figure holds a short sword in his right hand and appears to wear a *manica* on his right arm. Unfortunately, both the upper body of the gladiator and his opponent are missing in this portrayal, making it difficult to determine his type with certainty. But we can tentatively identify him as a *murmillo* or a *secutor* because of the *ocrea* and the *gladius*, which were typical of these gladiators. On his right, a table (?) holding a red vase is barely visible.

As noted above, the procession of the gladiators also continues on the side to the west of the entrance to room D (FIGURE 71). The first gladiator from

FIGURE 72.
Drawing of the predella at the end of corridor B.

FIGURE 73.
Depiction of a
Thracian. Suburban
Baths, Pompeii,
corridor B.

the east could be a *Thraex* (FIGURE 73). He is shown at three-quarters, turning towards the right. His face is completely covered by a helmet with a visor, adorned with red feathers. His right arm is protected by a *manica* that comes up almost to his shoulder. In his right hand he holds a *sica*, one of the identifying elements of this type, along with some *ocreae* that come up to the thighs on both legs. His opponent uses a long rectangular shield to protect himself, and only the yellow, cap-shaped helmet that covers his head is visible.

In the space above the predella, still more gladiatorial scenes appear on a white background, very damaged and full of lacunae due to the collapse of the wall and the plaster (FIGURE 74). The figures in this second area are larger

than the ones below. In the foreground, a gladiator lies on his back on the ground; his bent legs are protected by small dark leggings that come up to his calves. He wears a short white tunic, tightened around his waist by a red band, and carries a helmet with a visor. His left arm is bent and appears to hold a dark, curved object, very difficult to identify because of the poor condition of the fresco. At the time of the excavation, two figures fighting in the background were just barely visible on the top left of the fresco, along with a yellow circular shield, perhaps abandoned by the defeated gladiator.

FIGURE 74.
Predella and upper area with gladiatorial scenes. Suburban Baths, corridor B.

RICIO·A·FMEN
SCAVRO
II·VIR· ID
ECVRIONES·LOCVM·MONVM
XOOIN·FVNERE·ETPS̄TAT·VAM·E·VES·
ORO·PONENDAM·CENSVERVNT
SCAVRVS·PATER·FILIO

2. Paintings of Gladiators in Tombs

THE NECROPOLIS AT THE HERCULANEUM GATE: TOMB OF UMBRICIUS
SCAURUS   In the early nineteenth century, an important relief in painted
stucco, thought on the basis of an epigraph (*CIL* X.1024) to be connected to
the tomb of the *duovir* A. Umbricius Scaurus, was uncovered in the necropolis
at the Herculaneum Gate. Scenes of *venationes* and gladiatorial combat appear
in friezes, one above the other, decorating the high podium of the tomb. Of

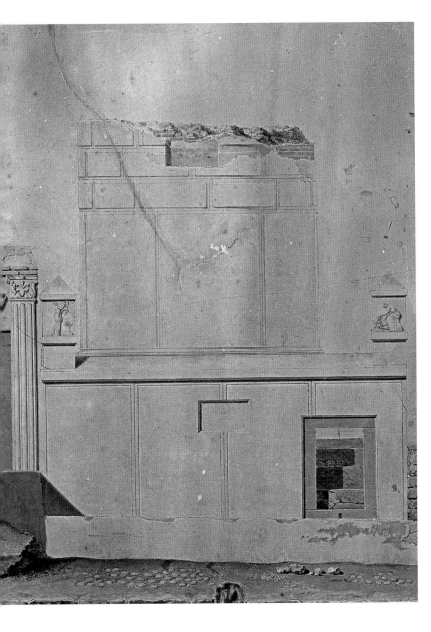

FIGURE 75.
Necropolis at the
Herculaneum Gate.
Drawing of the tomb
of Umbricius Scaurus
(ADS 1118).

this important cycle, only the drawings made by Mazois and Morelli at the
time of the excavation remain (FIGURE 75). A long frieze ran along the high
part of the funereal monument and above the doorway at the entrance to the
burial chamber. It represented eight pairs of gladiators involved in various
phases of combat. The gladiators' weapons were not shown; they may have
been fashioned in metal and appliquéd to the frieze separately. Consequently,
the types cannot be identified with certainty.

The first pair, reading from left to right, were *equites*, fighting on horseback. A pair of gladiators with similar armor followed, taking a break from combat. Next come a *hoplomachus* (?) and a *murmillo*; afterwards, a scene, not easy to interpret, showing two *secutores* in combat in the foreground, and two *retarii* in the background. The next pair comprises a Thracian and a *murmillo*. The frieze continued on the door and showed a *murmillo* being restrained by a man in a tunic (an assistant? a *lanista*?), followed by his defeated opponent, a Thracian. The last pair is composed of a victorious Thracian and his defeated opponent, a *murmillo*. As was very common for this kind of monument, the gladiator's name, the school to which he belonged, and the *pugnae* (fights) he had participated in, with their outcomes, were painted next to each gladiator. These facts show that the spectacle depicted actually took place. Above and beneath the gladiatorial frieze were scenes of a *venatio* with men who fought or goaded boars, lions, panthers, and bears.

This tomb dates back to the latter part of Nero's reign and the reign of Flavius. Above the depictions, a painted inscription referred to the gladiatorial games organized by Numerius Festius Ampliatus ("*Munere [N(umeri) Fes]ti Ampliati, die summo (pugnaverunt)*") (*CIL* IV.1182). Since it is difficult to correlate the *duovir* Umbricius Scaurus with the *editor muneris* Festius Ampliatus, it has been hypothesized that Scaurus's epigraph was placed on this tomb by mistake, and that the funeral monument belonged, in fact, to Numerius Festius Ampliatus, a famous organizer of gladiatorial spectacles. However, Sabbatini Tumolesi believes that the epigraph actually refers to the gladiatorial spectacle organized by Festius Ampliatus for the funeral of Umbricius Scaurus, in keeping with the very early, but not entirely vanished, practice of offering *munera* in homage to the deceased.

The Necropolis at the Vesuvian Gate: Tomb of Vestorius Priscus

Between 1907 and 1910, four sepulchral monuments were uncovered to the north of the Vesuvian Gate. Among them was the tomb of the aedile C. Vestorius Priscus, who died at the age of twenty-two. His mother, Mulvia Priscus, had the tomb built just before the eruption of A.D. 79. The tomb was made up of an altar on a high cubic pedestal, enclosed by a wall. Inside, a richly painted decoration still exists, which contrasts with the modest architecture of the monument. The paintings are partly decorative and partly allusions to episodes from the public and private life of the deceased. On the part of the wall to the left of the enclosure's entrance, a pair of gladiators is depicted on a dark red background (FIGURE 76). The one on the left, a *Thraex*, has defeated his opponent. He is leaning on his left leg, while his right leg is bent in front of him. In his left hand he has a shield; in his right hand, which is covered with a *manica*, he holds a weapon. Though no longer visible today, this was identified as a *sica* at the time of excavation. Draped over his *subligaculum* and torso, he wears a kind of

FIGURE 76.
Necropolis at the
Vesuvian Gate. Tomb
of Vestorius Priscus.
Fresco with gladiators.

transparent tunic, or a whitish-bluish veil. He has high leggings (*ocreae*), and his thighs are wrapped in bands adorned with various decorations. He wears a helmet with a wavy brim, perhaps ending in a griffin's head relief, and a wide yellow plume. A visor with eyeholes covers his face.

His opponent, generally identified as a *hoplomachus*, has fallen on his shield and is attempting to hold himself up with his left arm. In his right hand he appears to hold a dagger or a short sword (*gladius*). It is hard to tell whether he has a *manica* on his right arm. He wears short boots and a decorated band around his left knee. He also wears a *subligaculum*, held in place by a *balteus*, and his torso is covered by the same kind of transparent tunic as his opponent's. He wears a helmet with a wavy brim, an angular crest, and protection over his face. His sharply curved, rectangular shield and his helmet might classify this gladiator as a *murmillo*, rather than a *hoplomachus*.

On the adjoining wall of the enclosure, large cats chase other animals across a mountainous landscape. This painting, along with the representation of the gladiators, is thought to memorialize a *munus* organized by Vestorius Priscus when he was aedile.

RELIEF FROM THE NECROPOLIS AT THE STABIAN GATE   In 1843, outside of the Stabian Gate, excavations unearthed a rectangular funerary monument inscribed to the *duovir* Cn. or N. Clovatius and a marble relief with gladiatorial depictions (now at the Museo Archeologico Nazionale in Naples). In the same area, the remains of an inscription, now lost, recorded the spectacles in the amphitheater ordered by the magistrate A. Clodius Flaccus (*CIL* X.1074). Some scholars maintained that the relief belonged to the tomb of Clodius Flaccus, but others believed that it was connected to the funerary monument of Numerius Festinus Ampliatus, the best known *lanista* of Pompeii. The information recorded at the time of the excavation doesn't allow us to attribute the relief to either one of these figures with absolute certainty, and so the issue of the provenience and pertinence of the relief remains unresolved. It must date back to the reign of Tiberius.

The relief (1.5 × 4.23 m) is made up of two marble slabs that fit together (FIGURE 77). The pictorial episodes are arranged in three different spaces of varying heights, one above the other. The small ledge separating them also

FIGURE 77.
Relief from the necropolis at the Stabian Gate (A.D. 20–50). Naples, Museo Archeologico Nazionale (inv. 6704).

serves as a resting place for the figures. Three different moments of the *munus* are reproduced in the three spaces, in chronological order.

In the upper space, we see the opening ceremony, in which the *editor* himself examines the weapons (*probatio armorum*) (FIGURE 18). The parade opens at the right side with two lictors and three musicians. Following them is a group carrying a *ferculum*, or litter, on their shoulders, upon which two blacksmiths are seated, one in front of the other. According to Bianca Maiuri, this exposition of craft provided good publicity for those who produced the weapons. Next come the *harenarii* (the arena staff); the first carries a board indicating the date of the spectacle and the name of its *editor*, the second brings the palm destined for the victor. A figure in a toga follows, perhaps the *editor muneris* himself, and behind him is a line of *harenarii* bringing the helmets and shields to be used by the gladiators. The procession closes with a horn player and two *harenarii* holding the reins of horses, which are harnessed in style for the festivities.

In the middle space, five groups of gladiators engage in combat. The first group (left to right) is represented by two gladiators in tunics. The winner stands, raising his small circular shield in victory. His opponent, stretched out on the ground, still holds his sword and waits for the verdict. Since both gladiators are dressed alike, they must belong to the same category, probably the *equites*, who ended their combat on foot. The second group includes a victorious *murmillo*, who is waiting either to be proclaimed victor or to resume fighting. Beside him stands the referee. The defeated gladiator, a *Thraex*, is shown from behind, on his knees; he is supported by four assistants, while a fifth has collected his shield. The third group is represented by two gladiators with identical armor: the *subligaculum* and a scaled breastplate with a painting of a gorgon's head in the middle, held in place by two bands crossing in back. On their heads each wears a helmet with a short brim in front and a long brim behind, adorned by a plume. The left leg appears to be protected by a high legging, and the right hand by a *manica*. A comparison with other portraits—in particular, a relief with gladiators from the Museo Nazionale Romano (inv. 126119) (FIGURE 13)—suggests that the two combatants are *provocatores*. The fourth group pauses in the middle of combat. The gladiator on the left, held up by two *harenarii*, stretches out his wounded leg to be treated by a third *harenarius*. His opponent, also flanked by two assistants, prepares to drink from the cup being offered him. The *galerus* protecting the arm and left shoulder of both gladiators classifies them as *laquearii*. Little is known about this type of gladiator (Isidore of Seville *Origines* 18.56), but, like the *retiarius*, he seems to be furnished with a *galerus*. The last pair, like the second, consists of a *murmillo* and a *Thraex*, shown here in active combat. In this duel, however, it is the *Thraex* who strikes his opponent on the breastplate.

The area below the relief portrays scenes from a *venatio* with struggles between men and animals (a *bestiarius* and a bull, a *bestiarius* and a wild boar), as well as struggles among animals (a dog and a deer, a fawn and a bull, a dog and a wild boar). In the last scene, a bear, just out of the door, has already taken a bite out of a *bestiarius*, while two assistants, powerless, distance themselves with despairing gestures. The animals portrayed in these scenes from a *venatio* are probably ones that actually fought in the amphitheater at Pompeii. A fawn from the Apennines, a creature easy both to capture and to care for, was specifically mentioned in the programs of the *munera*.

NECROPOLIS AT THE NUCERIAN GATE: TOMB 2 EN   This tomb was explored in different phases in the mid-1950s. It is a burial chamber with an altar raised on a few steps, dating back to the latter period of Nero's or Flavius's reign. Inside, on a lunette, a young man dressed in a short tunic, armed with a dagger and a lance, is shown confronting a wild boar (FIGURE 78). Beneath the lunette, next to a niche, a great rectangular convex shield (*scutum*) is depicted. There are not enough epigraphic data to enable us to identify the tomb's occupant, but the pictorial data suggest that it is a gladiator. In other sites, such as Nîmes, necropoli of gladiators have been discovered not far from the amphitheater. Unfortunately, this has not occurred in Pompeii. In fact, the high density of ancient inhabitants right next to the amphitheater precludes the discovery of any necropoli there.

FIGURE 78.
Pompeii, necropolis at the Nucerian Gate, Tomb 2 EN.

3. The Paintings in Context

Although most of the paintings with gladiators at Pompeii have been lost, we can gather some interesting information from the descriptions made by the archaeologists who discovered them, and from the drawings made at the time of their excavation. These depictions were found in public buildings, funerary monuments, private houses, and taverns. But what was their function? Can they be considered simple decoration, or can they be attributed various functions, depending on the building from which they came? We have already seen that the gladiatorial paintings in the amphitheater were connected to the activities taking place there. But the function that these paintings had in funerary monuments is open for discussion. Some scholars maintain that these scenes alluded to the ancient custom of holding games at funerals, but this practice had already fallen off by the time the funerary reliefs in Pompeii were made.

Other scholars, in a more likely interpretation, see in these depictions the memory of spectacles that actually took place, thanks to the munificence of the deceased. These works would commemorate the generosity of a magistrate who had offered spectacles lavish enough to be immortalized on his own funerary monument. This interpretation would seem to be confirmed by the specific mention of the combatants' names and the outcomes of the contests, which occurs in the majority of these representations. Finally, a third hypothesis argues that the paintings held only a representational, not a funerary, content, like the same depictions in domestic contexts. Thus they served to cheer up the deceased, just as they had done during his lifetime. In any case, all of the hypotheses posit that the gladiatorial representations in the funerary sphere were connected to the urban elite.

On the other hand, the presence of gladiatorial paintings in houses and public buildings is believed to be the inverse of what we have just described for the tombs. Considered typical products of "popular art," such images would mark the houses in which they are found as lower-middle-class homes, if not homes of the gladiators themselves. In the same way, their presence in taverns or baths would indicate a lower-class clientele. In some taverns (IX 9.8 and IX 12.7), these representations were probably meant to recall the gladiators who lived in the neighborhood, but the issue becomes more complicated with the gladiatorial paintings in the domestic sphere.

In the private houses of Pompeii, gladiatorial paintings adorned mostly atriums (VIII 5.37; IX 9, d), vestibules (I 7.7), corridors (VIII 4.4), and peristyles (I 3.23; VIII 7.24). They were always somewhere near the entrance, or in transit areas, just as in Trimalchio's house in the *Satyricon*. These representations probably conformed to the taste of the patron and the fashion of the day. Their placement might indicate that, unlike the mythological paintings of Greek origin, their theme was not elevated enough for exhibition halls. Still, they satisfied the sensibility of the owner, who was perhaps more comfortable with themes that were intensely Roman, like amphitheater games. In any case, it would be risky to attempt to establish the owner's cultural grade or his affiliation to a certain social group based on the presence or absence of paintings on a gladiatorial theme. The taste for such images seems to have cut across all social classes in Pompeii. They appeared both in the houses of the urban elites and in more modest dwellings. Even outside of Pompeii, paintings with gladiators are found in widely dissimilar contexts. Gladiatorial paintings used as decor in villas and public buildings have been brought to light in France, the Low Countries, Germany, and Great Britain. Later these depictions were reproduced in mosaic, and they adorned the exhibition halls of important urban and rural residences, but this vogue began to spread only after Pompeii had already disappeared.

On the other hand, the practice of outfitting baths with scenes from the amphitheater was rather unusual. It has been suggested that their presence in the Suburban Baths in Pompeii is proof of the low social condition of this establishment's clientele. Still another hypothesis is possible: perhaps they evoked the spectacles that were so adored by the Pompeians at a time when people were prohibited from going to the amphitheater, following the riot in A.D. 59. Those who came to use the baths outside of the Marine Gate would have passed through the entrance hall, uplifted by the images of gladiatorial combat, where the weapons of the different categories were drawn with analytical precision and vivid colors. This spectacle, one of the usual pleasures of the clients at the Suburban Baths, must have resonated with nostalgia, if the cycle can be dated accurately to the period when gladiatorial shows at Pompeii were prohibited.

The corridor with the gladiator decor widened into a vestibule (as in FIGURE 68), where there were depictions of armed warriors, a typical theme in bathing establishments. Thus, in the Suburban Baths the traditional and ever-present motif of the Greek athlete fused with the motif of the new Roman athlete, the gladiator. The fact that the gladiator was now looked upon as a model is not so exceptional, and its equivalent is found in the contemporary literature. The gladiator's disdain for death and his manly courage explain his success and his ascent as a model, to a level on a par with more traditional heroes.

REPRESENTATIONS OF GLADIATORS: LAMPS, VASES, AND STATUES

The spectacles of the amphitheater constituted a particularly rich source of inspiration not only for painting and mosaic art but also for many other objects. In ceramic art, lamp disks decorated with individual gladiators, gladiatorial combat, and even mere designs of gladiatorial weapons were especially numerous. The reason for this success is fairly obvious. The lamp was an object used daily by every stratum of the population. To appeal to a large public, the lamp makers flooded the market with these images. Some of these scenes are very refined, and sometimes the figures are even accompanied by the names of the most famous champions of the day. The diffusion of these lamps is concentrated mostly in the first century A.D.; thereafter they gradually disappear, as a preference is shown for nonfigurative subjects. In Pompeii, lamps with gladiators were found in both tombs and houses (FIGURE 79).

Representations of gladiators were also reproduced on vases with relief decorations (see FIGURE 17), in imitation of fancy silver tableware that, as Petronius shows in the *Satyricon*, could display this kind of decoration. From Pompeii we have a bronze vessel (*situla*) of extraordinary artistry, on which two small figures of gladiators with locked shields have been applied in place

FIGURE 79.
Lamp decorated
with gladiators from
the House of Julius
Polybius. Pompeii,
Antiquarium
(inv. 21165).

FIGURE 80.
Bronze *situla* with
figurines of gladiators
applied in place of
handles. Naples, Museo
Archeologico Nazionale
(inv. 73146).

FIGURE 81, OPPOSITE
Bronze *tintinnabulum*
of a gladiator. Naples,
Museo Archeologico
Nazionale (inv. 27853).

of the handles (FIGURE 80). One unique bronze statuette belongs to a class of objects with an apotropaic function: a grotesquely rendered gladiator/*bestiarius* fights against his own phallus, which has been transformed into a panther (FIGURE 81). Bronze bells hang from the figure. These objects (*tintinnabula*) were hung at the entrances to houses and shops for good luck.

Terra-cotta statuettes of gladiators are rather rare. Two examples from the necropolis at the Herculaneum Gate, found in the so-called Tomb of the Blue Vase, are now in the Museo Archeologico Nazionale of Naples (FIGURE 82). Both statuettes depict a gladiator advancing toward the right, with *ocreae*, a loincloth, and a crested helmet. They both wear *manicae* and hold swords in their right hands. One gladiator holds a long rectangular shield, the other a small round shield (*parmula*). Two similar statuettes, one from the house of Marcus Lucretius (IX 3.5), are preserved at the Museo Archeologico Nazionale. They have been interpreted as votive offerings on the occasion of the Saturnalia, which were celebrated at the beginning of the new year. One interesting sculpture in tufa of a gladiator (1.21 m high) was found in the so-called Tavern of the Gladiator (I 20.1) (FIGURE 83). This building is

located in the vicinity of the amphitheater, not far from the Nucerian Gate. A tavern with its own vineyard, this type of establishment was quite common in the southeast area of Pompeii. To the left of the entrance, there is a basin for pressing grapes with the feet, a technique that produced an especially sweet and delicate wine. Beside it, four *dolia* (storage jars) were found, ready for the next harvest. In front of the basin is a *triclinium*—in antiquity, it was shaded by a pergola—on which one could lie down to eat and drink the innkeeper's wine. Amedeo Maiuri has hypothesized that the tavern was frequented mostly by those who crowded into the city from the farms and surrounding areas on game days. According to Maiuri, this would explain the presence of the gladiator statue, with its dually decorative and protective function. It could be a *hoplomachus*, with crested helmet, high leggings, and *subligaculum*. In his left hand he has a short straight sword, and in his right hand he raises a small round shield. To his right is the bearded Priapus, shown in his traditional pose; his cloak, laden with fruit, is lifted up to reveal a large phallus. Priapus is certainly an auspicious figure, a symbol of fertility, harvest, and wealth. His association with the gladiator is considered a further sign of divine protection. In Pompeii, there are other houses in which paintings of gladiators were connected to shrines (VIII 5.37; IX 3.13; IX 12.7); there too the intent may have been to augment the protective force.

In some houses, in addition to their commemorative and decorative function, the gladiatorial representations were probably meant to be auspicious. These images, evoking athletic-type victories or the palm branches so often represented in Pompeii, must have been regarded as symbols of good fortune for the household and its inhabitants. Therefore, the presence of images and representations of gladiators in houses, tombs, and shrines demonstrates not only how deeply passionate people were about these stars of the spectacle but also how complex and worthy of further study are both the function and value—even apotropaic—attributed to them.

FIGURE 82, PAGES 102–3
Terra-cotta statuettes of gladiators from the "Tomb of the Blue Vase" and the House of Marcus Lucretius, probably from the same source. Naples, Museo Archeologico Nazionale (inv. 20341).

FIGURE 83, OPPOSITE
Tufa statue of a gladiator from the so-called Tavern of the Gladiator. Pompeii, Antiquarium.

THE RIOT OF A.D. 59

Disturbances provoked by opposing fans of different champions or schools were not rare in the Roman world, but the riot that broke out in A.D. 59 in the amphitheater at Pompeii was serious enough to merit a record in the *Annales* of Tacitus (14.17).

Livineius Regulus, an ex-senator who had been expelled from the Senate by the emperor Claudius, organized some splendid games in the amphitheater at Pompeii, which the inhabitants of the nearby population centers rushed to see. According to Tacitus's account, discord broke out between the Pompeians and the Nucerians during the spectacle, provoked by an ordinary exchange of insults. From words followed deeds; stones were thrown, and then weapons were drawn. Since it was absolutely forbidden to carry weapons in public places, it is very likely that this was a premeditated attack. In fact, there had been bad blood between the Pompeians and the Nucerians, probably caused by border issues and a supposed violation of rights. Nuceria, unlike Pompeii, had remained faithful to Rome during the Social War, and in consequence was awarded the territory of Stabiae. This land grant must have been the primary cause of the quarrel between the two cities. The strengthening of the Nucerian colony through the introduction of new veterans, ordered by Nero in A.D. 57 (Tacitus *Annales* 13.31), just two years before the riot, only increased the tensions. While no trace of this bitterness appears in the passage by Tacitus, it does emerge in graffiti from Pompeii (*CIL* IV.1329, 2183, 1293). Tacitus continues his account of the riot by relating that the Pompeians were dominant in the struggle, and that many Nucerians were carried home either dead or mutilated.

News of the sorry incident reached Rome. The emperor asked the Senate to render a judgment, and the Senate charged the consuls with the investigation. Afterward, the Senate decided to exile all those who were implicated in the event, including the organizer of the games and the *duoviri* of that year— Pompeius Grosphus and Pompeius Grosphus Gavianus, father and adoptive son—and to shut down the amphitheater for ten years. However, the period of disqualification did not actually last that long. Scholars have proposed various hypotheses about when the games in the amphitheater were resumed, anywhere from a few months to five years afterwards.

From this mournful event, an extraordinary figurative document has been preserved, the fresco found in house I 3.23 (FIGURE 58). It represents the crucial moment of the clash: riotous groups are fighting in the arena and on the embankments, but the brawl has already moved outside, onto the walls and around the amphitheater, where itinerant vendors and simple passersby appear to carry on peacefully. In the painting, there is an acclamation to both Satrius Valens and Nero, which is considered highly significant. According to some scholars, it was D. Lucretius Satrius Valens, an eminent member of the Pompeian aristocracy, who interceded with Nero to revoke the amphitheater's disqualification after the catastrophic earthquake that struck Pompeii in A.D. 62. If the amphitheater could be reopened, and the games that were so important to the people could be resumed, the spirits of the Pompeians might be lifted a little, in the wake of such appalling devastation.

FROM THE GLADIATORS TO TIGER MAN

Knowledge, Confrontation, and Death in the Spectacle of the Duel

Riccardo Lattuada

A contest between two opponents, in front of an audience. This is the scheme, codified through a complex anthropological process, that lies at the heart of the gladiatorial aesthetic. The *Thraex*, the *murmillo*, the *Samnes*, and the *retiarius*, who fight according to a script of prearranged combat in an arena, constitute an allegory of the eternal conflict between different people. It is a confrontation that, in both Roman history and much of human history, is made up of conflicts and struggles, a mutual testing based on violence, and the measuring of one's own strength and ability against those of others. It is also based on the awareness of one's own weakness, and the weakness of others. Such a confrontation is, after all, a form of mutual knowledge—the most terrible kind, that which comes to fruition in war.

The ferocious and sensual ritual of the gladiator duels seems to have been constructed initially as the supreme reification of war, or rather, of wars. As if taken from an anthology of war stories and boiled down to single combat, the military campaigns of the Roman conquest are translated into metaphors that synthesize the encounters between Rome and its enemies as a contest between two individuals. Their armor, their weapons, and their shields are the chief symbols of this metaphorical struggle. As the power of Rome expanded to encompass Italy and ultimately the entire Western world, the gladiator games were no longer duels between equals, a celebration of two contestants matched in strength and ability. They became, instead, a reminder and an allegory of a long conflict with the peoples and traditions—military and civil—that Rome had conquered. (And wasn't this already the essence of the duel between the *Horatii* and the *Curiatii*?)

The expansion of Rome's power swelled the number of peoples it had subjugated. The *Samnes* recalled the victory over the Samnites, just as the *Thraex* recalled the victory over the Thracians. Thus, putting these actors in the arena at first symbolized their exorcism as the dreaded enemies, enemies who were only conquered at the price of incredible courage. To be sure, as enemies they

This piece is dedicated to the memory of Maurizio Fagiolo dell'Arco, and to the richness of his intellect and knowledge.

had shown great valor, but not as great as the victors'. It is no coincidence that when the Samnites became allies of Rome, and were thereby fully incorporated into the sphere of Roman culture, their costume was banned from the games. The enemy is exorcised when his living symbol is brought to fight in the arena, where, in the gladiatorial spectacle, history can occasionally be reversed. But a former enemy turned ally merits respect. Because he has lost his potential to inspire terror and anxiety, it would be disrespectful to reduce him as a meta-historical figure for the purpose of exorcism. Therefore, as the peoples inside the sphere of Rome were gradually conquered, the gladiators seemed decreasingly to embody their character as symbolic recollections of a real war between two peoples, two concepts of civilization, or two modes of affirming that civilization through the techniques and strategies of combat. For example, the female gladiators, another marvelous *monstruum* from the anthology of super-heroes of the Roman arena, might have been inspired by the myth of the Amazons. By the same token, the Ethiopian women whom Nero forced to fight in honor of the Armenian king Tiridates must have symbolized their distance from the Roman world. Mevia, whom Juvenal pictures in the arena fighting boars with spear in hand and breasts exposed, is like the reincarnation of Diana. And so, more than history, the law of nature (*murmillo* versus *retiarius*, combatants versus beasts), or myth (the Ethiopian women, or Mevia), gradually became the backdrop for the symbolic references to the gladiatorial spectacles in their period of codification.

The gladiatorial spectacle gradually turned into an anthology of clashes, two combatants at a time, in which the symbols incarnated by the gladiators met once again on the abstract level of the duel, equalized by the rules and context of the conflict. The gladiators' rise to stardom, in the midst of so many fans and opposing allegiances, transferred the significance of their public personae into their lives as individuals. In a society as complex and highly literate as Rome, the extraordinary amount of epigraphic material and written texts still known to us today allows us to glimpse *in nuce* the first processes of meditation on their spectacles and the creation of certain customs that are deeply ingrained in our social life today. The gladiatorial contests were popular in the broadest sense of the word: the combat between famous gladiators was a duel between stars, and their way of fighting was, in itself, an exercise in style and taste—if one may apply such terms to physical combat.

Beginning with the gladiatorial games, the spectacularization of the duel took a secular direction, assuming different forms with each age. In the Middle Ages, the chivalric epic, with its rules, duels, and heroes, was destined to effect a narrower social sector, regulated by rituals that are more diversified than those of the gladiatorial spectacles of the Roman world. In the Middle Ages, there was plenty of violence, mostly associated with war, but there was no Roman state system to universalize laws, institutions, customs, and even the forms of social violence. Other ideas lay at the heart of the codified duel in the context of the knightly tournament. The king or lord attended the duels together with the common people. The abilities of the contenders were expressed not so much in the physical conflict for the defense of one's honor—

a typical medieval concept—as in the selection of the best knights to the service of their sovereign. The theater of the tournament was no longer the Roman amphitheater, but the castle court or the exercise field near the city walls. And the entire context of the knightly tournament was more circumscribed, more local, and far less secular and cross-class than the spectacular, meticulous, and universalizing show business of the Romans.

In this phase of Western civilization, the spectacle of the duel often centered on the confrontation between religious enemies: consider the clashes between Christian knights and Muslims beneath the walls of Jerusalem, later transfigured into the mythic duels of *Gerusalemme Liberata*. Christianity found in the knight a symbol of the secular martyr, despite the fierce and often amoral attitudes of those who incarnated this figure. Moreover, the idea of bringing together in a knightly order all those who possessed the same qualities of faith, integrity, and courage was born in this period; for example, the Knights Templars, who were joined together under the emblem of the Shroud, a coat-of-arms that defended faith, courage, and military discipline. This ancient gladiator costume was made into a uniform, the symbol of an elite corps holding shared religious ideals, and belonging to the same social class, as well as sharing the same training in the arts of dueling and war. Their goals were not at all sporting, even though they did participate in tournaments. War was the final objective, and the ritualization of conflict through the tournament and training was the exact opposite of what it was in Rome. There, the spectacle was the allegory of war; here, it was preparation and forearming for war, if not its realization.

The strength of this tradition passed from the Middle Ages to the Early Modern period. In the commingling of classical and medieval traditions that marked so much of the Nordic quattrocentro, the tournament still occupied a place of importance. Even the youth of Charles V was characterized by public displays of courage in the tournaments between Flemish and Burgundian knights, in whose company the future Holy Roman emperor grew up. And precisely by virtue of these medieval traditions, still alive during the late Middle Ages, the cult of the knight found its *emblemata* in the colors and signs of the coats-of-arms. Symbols of caste, family, and history, coats-of-arms had by the first half of the fifteenth century become both projection and apex of the legendary images in the Sala baronale of the Castello della Manta, near Saluzzo. Hung from the trees that define the backdrop behind the kings and warriors, the Sala baronale coats-of-arms reverberate in the heraldic decor of the costumes and arms of their owners. The difference between Godfrey de Bouillon or Charlemagne and the Roman *retiarius* or *Samnes* is considerable; the latter were secular figures associated only with the gladiatorial spectacle, except to the extent that they distinguish themselves as stars of their own specialty in the mind of the public.

In the Renaissance, the gladiatorial games moved from the domain of fact to the dimension of myth: Charles V, anxious to assert himself as the new universal emperor, did everything he could to deprive his most powerful and hawkish lords of their status as first among equals. But precisely because the

FIGURE 84.
Paris Bordone,
Battle of the Gladiators,
ca. 1560. Vienna,
Kunsthistorisches
Museum.

Colosseum and other Roman amphitheaters were symbols of the myth of classicism—vitally stimulating to the intellectuals of the day—the vestiges of these buildings spurred the erudite to reconstruct not only the antiquity of the *ludi* but also their rituals. Onofrio Panvinio (1529–1568), an Augustinian father from Verona, was a cultured antiquarian, beloved by bibliophiles. His work, *De Ludis Circensibus*, published posthumously in 1570 and reprinted several times during the seventeenth century, was the first systematic collation of gladiator material, presenting itself as an ideal sequel to *The Triumphs of Caesar*, which Andrea Mantegna painted for Francesco Gonzaga in the last decade of the fifteenth century. Panvinio's detailed antiquarian research reconstructed more or less exactly the arena, the combatants, and the architectonic and functional contexts of the gladiatorial games.

It is probably no coincidence that the revival of the gladiatorial myth would soon produce works with specific imagery. For example, *Battle of the Gladiators* by Paris Bordone in the Kunsthistorisches Museum in Vienna (ca. 1560), an immense scene measuring 2.18 by 3.29 meters, clearly accords with Du Pérac's prints for Panvinio's book (FIGURE 84). Here, the myth of Rome is synthesized across a wide boulevard—as abstract as in De Chirico's work centuries later—along whose sides a mental anthology of the city's most famous monuments reveals itself: on the right, the Septizonium, the Pantheon, the Trajan Column, all the way to Augustus's Egyptian obelisk; on the left, the Hadrianeum and the Colosseum. In the center of this imaginary city, several combatants fight simultaneously, barely separated from the public by a parti-

tion, as if the games had been moved from the amphitheater to the street: could this be an abstract restitution of the Forum? Works like this one by Bordone are the expression and foundation of the culture of a great deal of secular classicism. It would be more widely employed later, with an expanded visual repertory—not only in Venice, where the first edition of *De Ludis Circensibus* was printed, but also and especially in Rome. Without it, the works of certain forerunners of classicism—Nicolas Poussin, Pietro Testa, Giacinto Gimignani, and Pietro da Cortona—would be unthinkable.

The works of Panvinio and Bordone become important sources for the renaissance of the myth of the *ludi* and the gladiators, culminating in the paintings at the Casón del Buen Retiro in Madrid, commissioned by Count Duke Olivares. Here, in the summer residence of Philip IV, a complex web of symbolic allusions was meant to show the classical and imperial ascendance of the Spanish dynasty. Some of the works—ordered in great haste during the 1640s—were meant to evoke the magnificence of the Spanish conquest, such as the famous *Surrender of Breda* of Velazquez (c. 1635), now at the Prado, which was painted for the Buen Retiro. But the themes of the *otia* (leisure) and the *ludi* characterize a large part of the works commissioned between Rome and Naples. Thus, *Gladiators Fighting at a Banquet* by Giovanni Lanfranco (1637–40; FIGURE 85) and the famous works by Neapolitan artists like Aniello Falcone, Micco Spadaro, Andrea de Lione, Viviano Codazzi, and others were created. The so-called *Gladiators* by Falcone at the Prado (ca. 1635–40), now more appropriately called *Wrestlers* (*Lottatori*), is a parade of nude athletes

FIGURE 85.
Giovanni Lanfranco,
*Gladiators Fighting
at a Banquet*, 1637–40.
Madrid, Museo del
Prado.

involved in a melancholic conversation beneath the statue of Victory. The athlete's destiny is tied to this statue: Fate will decide the outcome of the contest, taking precedence over his ability and physical virtues. A neo-Stoic patina now colors the aesthetic of the duel and the conflict. In the immense series of canvases for the Buen Retiro, the new emperor, Philip IV, is celebrated as he returns to the classicism of the Roman games. The gladiators and their activities are one of the elements of this celebration, and classicism as exemplum is an experiential field that will reverberate as the myth of the gladiators evolves.

The heroic eighteenth century, better suited to rediscovering the moral lessons of classical antiquity, rarely explored the topos of the duel. Yet, when it did so, the outcome was excellent, as in the *Death of Consul Lucius Junius Brutus* by Giambattista Tiepolo in the Kunsthistorisches Museum in Vienna (ca. 1725–30). In the eighteenth century, the aesthetic of the duel was, first and foremost, an allegory of moral redemption. In *Les Liaisons dangereuses* (1782) by Pierre Choderlos de Laclos, Valmont, absolute canon of amorality, stoically pays for the suffering he has inflicted in the complex geometry of his relationships by dying in a duel and peacefully redeeming his life. The duel is no longer a spectacle but the allegory of a moral encounter. Its function—narrative and figurative—is no longer the spectacular exorcism of a defeated enemy and the fears he aroused, but a dramatic, ritualized encounter between various types of existence, ways of life, and ethical models. The two complex characters in Ridley Scott's film *The Duelists* (1977) obey the same logic, and its historic context—the Napoleonic wars—is no coincidence: the challenger continually seeks out conflict, and the pursued one flees in vain. Yet when the latter prevails in the final encounter, he decrees the death of his opponent: not his physical death, but rather his obsessive rival's obligation to disappear from his life. This story is similar in many ways to Heinrich von Kleist's *The Duel* (1881), a drama in which the conflict plays out on different levels, including violence, but mostly as a kind of mental strategizing, in a continuous upending of moral roles.

The nineteenth century proved to be strongly indebted to this vision, drawing out its more pathetic aspects: *Pollice verso* (Thumbs Down) by Jean-Léon-Gérôme (1872) is a tragic theatrical epilogue (FIGURE 21). The victor's gleaming helmet, every detail of his weapons, the velarium over the arena, the architecture—they are all defined by a sharp visual vocabulary that gives life to the museum objects that the painter observes with the precision of an archaeological illustrator. The viewer sees neither the victor's face nor that of the vanquished. We can only perceive, in the perfection of the shadows that the velarium casts over the arena, the shaped diptych of the two figures: one on the ground, the other on his feet, both united in the passive acceptance of the verdict. Gérôme dramatizes the experience of the gladiatorial game as a sad allegory of destiny, and with his extraordinary painting, he prepares a guiding image for the vast production of sword-and-sandal movies that unfolds over much of the twentieth century.

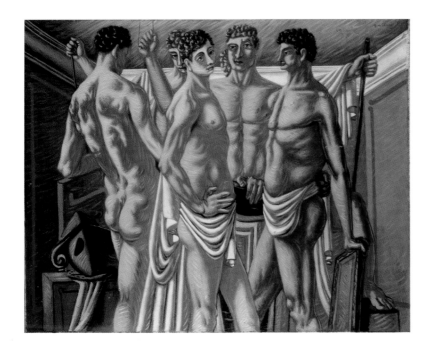

FIGURE 86.
Giorgio De Chirico,
Gladiators, 1928.
Private collection.

But before moving on to this aspect of twentieth-century art, we must look at some of the paintings that, in the eternal return to classicism, treat the theme of the gladiators. On February 27, 1928, Arrigo Boito's *Nerone* was performed for the inauguration of the Teatro Reale dell'Opera in Rome. Duilio Cambellotti's scenography revisited the gladiatorial theme with some sketches of remarkable freshness. Boito's allegory found a new way to express certain images. The physicality of the gladiator's bodies, rather than their attributes as combatants, became the focus. Paradoxically, this made the costumes less historically accurate than they had been all the way up to, and including, Gérôme. With Cambellotti, the bodies of the athletes were more important than their armor, like the statues of the Stadio Olimpico in Rome. The more literal and literary classicism of the nineteenth century had been consumed in an atemporal and existential vision, which, from a figurative point of view, had little to do with history.

The purely historical and literal interpretation of the gladiator's image eventually reaches its end, and this is nowhere better represented than in an extraordinary, but little known, figurative cycle. In the same year that Cambellotti produced scenery and costumes for Boito's *Nerone*, Giorgio De Chirico was commissioned by the cultured collector Leonce Rosenberg to create a series of gladiator paintings, to be hung in a Room of the Gladiators especially prepared in the collector's Parisian home. The series was dispersed in 1960, but we are familiar with almost all of its elements; ten of the paintings are known to us from photographs. Between 1928 and 1930, De Chirico produced numerous variations on the theme of gladiators, all connected to studies that he made for Rosenberg's Room of the Gladiators.

In the Rosenberg series, De Chirico attains one of his personal heights, and he celebrates the myth of the gladiators in what is probably the most complex pictorial cycle dedicated to this theme in twentieth-century art. The gladiators, mostly naked, occupy almost all of the figurative space, like live statues (FIGURE 86). In distinguishing his gladiators, De Chirico limits his use of scholarly resources: helmets, lances, and daggers create the context, along with a few other archaeological vestiges. The bare spatial contexts are modern, as if the arena had been transferred from the amphitheater to a private bourgeois apartment of the twentieth century. Some of the figures are immobile; in slightly dejected postures, they hold their weapons loosely, creating an image of interior defeat. In some dagger duels, the faces of the figures are hidden by their helmets. In some cases, De Chirico's familiar mannequin motif is transfigured in faces absent of any features, yet still human.

In the unsettling *Gladiators at Rest* from the Rosenberg series, a fighter is seated on a stool, his helmet on the ground, looking at the viewer with empty eyes. He doesn't even seem to expect an answer to his unknowable questions. In this series, De Chirico constructs a closed epos of emotional, familial, and bourgeois relationships, in which the protagonists' conditions of struggle or repose are allegories of emotional and existential conflicts. It represents an apex in his work. The theme of the gladiators is a starting point for a subtle hermeticism. The bodies of his warriors confront one another, they clutch at one another, and they oppose one another with a mute, inexpressive, and unappeased sorrow, reminiscent of the poems of Montale. In some groups, the bronzed skin is like the clay of an Etruscan sculpture, and the homoerotic vein that runs through the whole cycle is cloaked in an inscrutable solemnity.

But only when we move from the artistic avant-garde of the twentieth century to the mobile world of mass media does the ancient heritage of the gladiators return and take up the project of recovering the Roman rituals. From the myth of the gladiator as a kind of yearning for freedom, celebrated in Stanley Kubrick's *Spartacus* (1960), to the postmodern duels of *Rollerball* (1975), and finally to Ridley Scott's *Gladiator* (2000), the Roman setting is a metahistorical field of action, and its characters are still tied to a romantic vision. If the ending of *Gladiator* has no historical basis whatsoever—a gladiator who kills the emperor in the arena!—the good guy and the bad guy, set against each other in their final, titanic encounter, express, in its most extreme form, the confrontation between human beings, culminating in the death of both protagonists. And the myth lives on in an infinite number of popular forms, which reify everyday violence. The sport of wrestling, with its athlete-wrestler-actors dressed in superhero costumes, is a tribute to the logic of *panem et circenses*. Now the arena is televised, and the costumes of the combatants are lifted from the heroes of Marvel comic books (the Hulk, Spiderman, and their enemies) in a kind of hyperrealistic theatrical show. And the spectators cheer for the actors with whom they identify on an emotional and existential level.

These schemes even fuel the entertainment of adolescents. In Japanese cartoons, robot heroes manipulate prodigious technological prostheses, capable of transforming their physical essence (Marshall McLuhan's perfect negative allegory). A whole saga of champions comes to life, and they clash in the arena in a struggle in which human heroism emerges as a moral element to triumph over unheard-of forms of corporeal enhancement. The values of the good guy, his capacity to find exceptional strength within himself despite the superhuman powers of his adversaries, are colored with a slightly gloomy existentialism. Tiger Man, engaged in a solitary epic of conflicts with ferocious and powerful monsters, is an isolated figure, living only for the love of an audience who knows nothing of his existential travails.

Thus, our spectacles continue to reassert, with full force, the mystery of people coming to know other people in the codified forms of the modern duel. It is a knowledge made of violence and death. But in a way that is as paradoxical as it is ingrained in us, it is also a source of inexhaustible passion and love. To return to De Chirico, and a sentence painted on one of his works: *Et quid amabo nisi quod aenigma est?* (What shall I love, if not that which is an enigma?) We still need our gladiators.

BIBLIOGRAPHY

General References

Les Gladiateurs, exh. cat. (Musée Archéologique de Lattes, 1987); *Spectacula I. Gladiateurs et amphithéâtres*, Proceedings of the Colloquium at Toulouse and Lattes, 26–29 May 1987 (1990); AA.VV., *Sangue e arena*, Martellago (VE) 2001; R. Angelone, "Spettacoli gladiatori ad Ercolano e gli edifici da essi postulati," *Rendiconti dell'Accademia di Archeologia, Lettere e Belle Arti di Napoli*, n.s. 62 (1989–90; published 1992), pp. 215–43; F. Coarelli, "Il rilievo con scene gladiatorie," *Studi Miscellanei* 10 (1966), pp. 85–99; F. Dupont, "Gli spettacoli," *Storia di Roma dall'antichità ad oggi. Roma antica*, A. Giardina, ed. (Rome and Bari, 2000), pp. 281–306; D. Faccenna, "Rilievi gladiatori," *Bullettino della Commissione Archeologica Comunale di Roma* 73 (1949–50), pp. 3–14; M. Fora, *I munera gladiatoria in Italia: Considerazioni sulla loro documentazione epigrafica* (Naples, 1996); A. Gabucci, ed., *The Colosseum* (Los Angeles, 2001); M. Junkelmann, *Das Spiel mit dem Tod. So Kämpfen Roms Gladiatoren* (Mainz am Rhein, 2000); E. Köhne and C. Ewigleben, eds., *Gladiators and Caesars* (Berkeley, 2000); D. Mancioli, *Giochi e Spettacoli. Vita e costumi dei Romani antichi* 4 (Rome, 1987); P. J. Meier, *De gladiatura romana quaestiones selectae* (Bonn, 1881); M. G. Mosci Sassi, *Il linguaggio gladiatorio* (Bologna, 1992); A. Varone, "I giochi e gli spettacoli," *Bellezza e lusso. Immagini e documenti di piaceri della vita* (Rome, 1992); P. Veyne, *Il pane e il circo: Sociologia storica e pluralismo politico* (Bologna, 1984); C. W. Weber, *Panem et circenses: La politica dei divertimenti di massa nell'antica Roma* (Milan, 1989).

On Spartacus

D. Foraboschi, "La rivolta di Spartaco," *Storia di Roma 2, L'impero mediterraneo. I. La repubblica imperiale* (Turin, 1990), pp. 715–23; A. Guarino, *Spartaco. Analisi di un mito* (Naples, 1979); A.V. Mishulin, *Spartacus. Abriss der Geschichte des grossen Sklavenaufstandes* (Berlin, 1952); G. Stampacchia, *La tradizione della guerra di Spartaco da Sallustio a Orosio* (Pisa, 1976).

On the amphitheaters

Anfiteatro Flavio. Immagine Testimonianze Spettacoli (Rome, 1988); J.-C. Golvin, *L'amphithéâtre romain. Essai sur la théorisation de sa forme et de ses fonctions* (Paris, 1988); P. Gros, *L'architecture romaine du début du IIIe siècle av. J.C. à la fin du Haupt-Empire, 1. Les monuments publics* (Paris, 1996); L. Spina, *L'anfiteatro campano di Capua* (Naples, 1997).

On the division of places in the entertainment venues

J. Formigé, "Remarques diverses sur le théâtres romains à propos de ceux d'Arles et d'Orange," *Mémoires présentés par divers savants à l'Académie des Inscriptions et Belles-Lettres* 13 (1923); J. Kolendo, "La répartition des places aux spectacles et la stratification sociale dans l'Empire Romain. À propos des inscriptions sur les gradins des amphithéâtres et théâtres," *Ktema* 6 (1981), pp. 301–15.

On the tickets for entertainment venues

A. Degrassi, *Inscriptiones Latinae liberae rei publicae* (Florence, 1963), pp. 257–78; G. Henzen, "Tessere ed altri monumenti in osso," *Annali Inst. di Corrisp. Arch.* 20 (1848); R. Herzog, *Aus der Geschichte des Bankwesens im Altertum: Tesserae nummulariae* (Giessen, 1919); L. Pedroni, "Tessere da una collezione privata," *Archeologia Classica* 47 (1995), pp. 161ff.

On the velarium and other amenities

G. Cozzo, "Il velario negli antichi edifici anfiteatrali," *Archeologia Classica* 47 (1995), p. 196ff; G. B. Giovenale, "Erunt vela," *Atti II Congr. St. Rom.* 1 (1931), p. 181ff; R. Graefe, *Vela erunt* (Mainz am Rhein, 1979); A. Scobie, "Spectator Security and Comfort at Gladiatorial Games," *Nikephoros* 1 (1988), pp. 191–243.

On the gladiatorial games at Pompeii

R. Minervini, "Di un programma di gladiatori in Pompei," *Rivista illustrata* 4, 30 (June 1881), pp. 2–4; W. O. Moeller, "Gnaeus Alleius Nigidius Maius princeps coloniae," *Latomus* 32 (1973), pp. 515–20; J. Overbeck and A. Mau, *Pompeji in seinen Gebäuden, Alterthümern und Kunstwerken dargestellt*, 4th ed. (Leipzig, 1884); P. Sabbatini Tumolesi, *Gladiatorum paria. Annunci di spettacoli gladiatorii a Pompei* (Rome, 1980).

On gladiatorial graffiti

F. M. Avellino, "Osservazioni su talune iscrizioni e disegni graffiti sulle mura di Pompei," *Memorie della Real Accademia di Archeologia* 5 (1846), pp. 47–80; L. Canali and G. Cavallo, *Graffiti latini. Scrivere sui muri a Roma antica* (Milan, 1998); K. M. Coleman, "A Left-handed Gladiator at Pompeii," *Zeitschrift für Papyrologie und Epigraphik* 114 (1996), pp. 194–96; E. Diehl, *Pompeianische Wandinschriften und Verwandtes*, 2nd ed. (Berlin, 1930); C. Giordano, *La gens Cominia in Nola e il suo contributo alla colonizzazione dell'Africa Romana. (Spettacoli anfiteatrali in Nola e l'origine della città di Comiziano alla luce dei graffiti pompeiani)* (1979); W. Krenkel, *Pompejanischen Inschriften* (Heidelberg, 1963); F. P. Maolucci Vivolo, *Pompei. I graffiti figurati* (Foggia, 1993); A. Mau, "Iscrizioni gladiatorie di Pompei," *RM* 5 (1890), pp. 38ff; H. Solin, "Le iscrizioni parietali," *Pompei 79. Raccolta di studi per il decimonono centenario dell'eruzione vesuviana*, F. Zevi, ed. (Naples, 1979), pp. 278–88; V. Väänänen, *Graffiti di Pompei e di Roma* (Rome, 1962); A. Varone, *Erotica pompeiana* (Rome, 1994).

On the amphitheater at Pompeii and its paintings

Pompei 1748–1980. I tempi della documentazione, exh. cat. (Rome, 1981), pp. 36–37, 184–85; J. W. Goethe, *Italienische Reise* (Naples, 1989), pp. 381, 421, fig. 162; M. Della Corte, *Pompei, gli ultimi scavi e l'anfiteatro* (Pompeii, 1931); R. Garrucci, "Epoca in che fu costruito l'Anfiteatro pompeiano," *Bull. Arch. Nap.* (1853), n. 19, pp. 145–48; M. Girosi, "L'anfiteatro di Pompei," *Memorie Acc. Arch. Lettere e Belle Arti di Napoli* 5 (1936), p. 29ff; F. Niccolini, *Le case e i monumenti di Pompei disegnati e descritti* 3, no. 1 (Naples, 1854–96); G. Spano, *Alcune osservazioni nascenti da una descrizione dell'anfiteatro di Pompei* (Naples, 1953); *Rivista di Studi Pompeiani* 4 (1990), pp. 45–124; *PPM* 9, p. 31; pp. 106–11; p. 1008, fig.1.

On the riot of A.D. 59

F. Blumenthal, "Praefectus I.D.," *Hermes* 44 (1909), pp. 625–28; H. Galsterer, "Politik in römischen Städten: die 'seditio' des Jahres 59 n. Ch. in Pompei," *Studien zur antiken Sozialgeschichte. Festschrift für Friedrich Vittinghoff* (Cologne and Vienna, 1980), pp. 323–38; E. Magaldi, "I judicia Augusti e la rissa dell'Anfiteatro," *Rivista di Studi Pompeiani* (1936); A. Maiuri, "Pompei e Nocera," *Rendiconti dell'Accademia di Archeologia Lettere e Belle Arti di Napoli*, n.s. 33 (1958; published 1959), pp. 35–40; W. O. Moeller, "The Riot of A.D. 59 at Pompeii," *Historia* 19 (1970), pp. 90ff; H. Mouritsen, *Elections, Magistrates, and Municipal Elite: Studies in Pompeian Epigraphy* (Rome, 1988), esp. p. 35 and nn. 143, 148.

On the Gladiators' Barracks (V 5.3)

I. R. Curtius, "A Slur on Lucius Asicius the Pompeian Gladiator," *Transactions of the American Philological Association* 110 (1980), pp. 51–60; A. Mau, *RM* 16 (1901), pp. 288–312; idem, "Iscrizioni gladiatorie di Pompei," *RM* 5 (1890), pp. 25–39, 64–65; A. Sogliano, *NSc* (1899), pp. 228–35, 347–57; idem, "Il primitivo ludo gladiatorio di Pompei," *Rendiconti dell'Accademia dei Lincei*, ser. 5, 30 (1921), pp. 17–29.

On the Ludus gladiatorius (VIII 7.16)

Museo Borbonico 5 (Naples, 1829), pls. 10–11; R. Garrucci, "Il 'Ludus Gladiatorius', overo Convito dei Gladiatori in Pompei," *Bull. Arch. Nap.*, n.s. 1 (1853), n. 13, pp. 98–104, pl. 7, 5; idem, "Dell'arma gladiatoria detta 'Galerus'," *Bull. Arch. Nap.*, n.s. 1 (1853), n. 13, pp. 101–4 and n. 15, p. 113; idem, "Di due trofei di armi scoperti in Pompei al 1767 nel 'Ludus Gladiatorius' e della 'Sica' o falcetta dei Treci," *Bull. Arch. Nap.*, n.s. 1 (1853), n. 15, pp. 114–15; idem, "Nuovi programmi pompeiani appartenenti a spettacoli gladiatori," *Bull. Arch. Nap.*, n.s. 1 (1853), n. 15, pp. 115–17; G. Minervini, "Caserma dei Gladiatori," *Bull. Arch. Nap.*, n.s. 7 (1859), n. 165, pp. 116–20.

On the *Schola armaturarum* (III 3.6)

M. Della Corte, *Iuventus. Un nuovo aspetto della vita pubblica di Pompei finora inesplorato, studiato e ricostruito sulla scorta dei relativi documenti epigrafici, demografici, artistici e religiosi* (Arpino, 1924); V. Spinazzola, *NSc* (1916).

On the depictions of gladiators at Pompeii

J. M. Croisille, *Poesie et art figuré de Néron aux Flaviens* (Brussels, 1982); B. M. Felletti Maj, *La tradizione italica nell'arte romana* (Rome, 1977); T. Fröhlich, *Lararien und Fassadenbilder in den Vesuvstädten. Untersuchungen zur 'volkstümlichen' pompeianischen Malerei* (Mainz, 1991); W. Helbig, *Die Wandgemälde der vom Vesuv verschütteten Städte Campaniens* (Leipzig, 1868); V. Iorio, *La decorazione pittorica in contesti funerari: l'esempio di Pompei* (in press); F. Mazois, *Les ruines de Pompéi*, vols. 1–4 (Paris, 1824–38); Y. Perrin, "Un témoignage de Pline sur l'evolution socio-culturelle de son temps (*NH* 35, 52)," *Pline l'Ancienne temoin de son temps. Conventus pliniani internationalis Namneti*, 22–26 October 1985 (Salamanca and Nantes, 1987), pp. 385ff.; S. Reinach, *Répertoire des peintures greques et romaines* (Paris, 1922); K. Schefold, *Die Wände Pompejis. Topographisches Verzeichnis der Bildmotive* (Berlin, 1957); A. Sogliano, "Le pitture murali campane scoverte negli anni 1867–1879," *Pompei e la regione sotterrata dal Vesuvio nel anno 79*, 2 (Naples, 1879), pp. 87–243.

On the paintings in the House of Anicetus (I 3.23)

PPM 1 (1990), pp. 77–78; M. Della Corte, *Case ed abitanti di Pompei*, 3rd ed. (Naples, 1965), pp. 267–68; A. Donati, ed., *Romana Pictura. La pittura romana dalle origini all'età bizantina* (Venice, 1998); G. de Petra, "L'anfiteatro pompeiano rappresentato in un antico dipinto," *GdS* 1 (1868), n. 8; (1869), cc. 185–87; G. Fiorelli, *Gli scavi di Pompei dal 1861 al 1872* (Naples, 1873) p. 74; idem, *Descrizione di Pompei* (Naples, 1875), p. 56A; Fröhlich, *Lararien und Fassadenbilder*, pp. 241–47; F. Matz, *BdI* (1869), pp. 240–42; Reinach, *Répertoire des peintures*, 285, 5; Schefold, *Die Wände Pompejis*, p. 12; A. Sogliano, *Le pitture murali campane*, (Naples, 1879), nn. 604, 665, 666; T. Schreiber, *Kulturhistorischer Bilderatlas* 1 (Leipzig, 1885), pl. 28, 3, 4; G. Wataghin Cantino, "Veduta dall'alto e scena a volo d'uccello," *Rivista dell'istituto nazionale d'archeologia e storia dell'arte*, n.s. 16 (1969), pp. 52–53; F. Zevi, "L'arte popolare," *La pittura di Pompei* (Milan, 1991), pp. 267–73.

On the tavern in I 4.27

Schefold, *Die Wände Pompejis*, p. 17; Sogliano, "Le pitture murali campane," n. 667.

On the House of D. Octavius Quartius (II 2.2–5)

PPM 3 (1991), p. 108; M. Della Corte, *NSc* (1927), pp. 115ff; idem, *NSc* (1939), p. 313; A. Maiuri, *NSc* (1939), 197, 1; V. Spinazzola, *Pompei alla luce degli scavi nuovi di Via dell'Abbondanza (anni 1910–1923)* 1 (Rome, 1953), p. 415.

On the House of the Sacerdos Amandus (I 7.7)

Della Corte, *Case ed abitanti di Pompei*, pp. 314–15; Felletti Maj, *La tradizione italica*, p. 118; J. Kolendo, "Uno Spartaco sconosciuto nella Pompei osca: le pitture della casa di Amando," *Index* 9 (1980), pp. 33–40; E. La Rocca and M. and A. de Vos, *Guida archeologica di Pompei* (Verona, 1976), p. 211; K. Lehmann-Hartleben, "Ein historisches Gemälde in Pompeji," *Forschungen und Fortschritte* 4, no. 3 (1928), p. 21ff; A. Maiuri, "Relazione sui lavori di scavo dal marzo 1924 al marzo 1926," *Pompei. Nuovi scavi nella via dell'Abbondanza, NSc* 3 (1927), p. 21, fig. 5; idem, "Le pitture delle case di 'M. Fabius Amandio', del 'sacerdos Amandus' e di 'P. Cornelius Teges,'" *Monumenti della pittura antica scoperti in Italia 3. Le pitture ellenistico romane. Pompei* 2 (1938), pp. 3–5, fig. 5a, b; S. Mishulin, *Spartacus*, pp. 82–84; *PPM* 1 (1990), p. 588; Schefold, *Die Wände Pompejis*, p. 30; G. Spano, *Campania Felice* (Naples, 1941), p. 275; Stampacchia, *La tradizione della guerra di Spartaco*, pp. 120–22.

On the tavern in VII 4.26

PPM. L'immagine di Pompei nei secoli XVIII e XIX (Rome, 1995), p. 120; Fiorelli, *Descrizione di Pompei*, p. 216; Reinach, *Répertoire des peintures*, 285–86; Mazois, *Les ruines de Pompéi* 4, 48; Schreiber, *Kusturhistorischer Bilderatlas*, pl. 30, 10; H. Thédenat, *Pompéi. Histoire. 2. Vie publique* (Paris, 1906), p. 97; R. Cagnat and V. Chapot, *Manuel d'archéologie romaine* 2 (Paris, 1920), p. 127; Schefold, *Die Wände Pompejis*, p. 176; Helbig, *Die Wandgemälde*, n. 1516; Overbeck and Mau, *Pompeji in seinen Gebäuden*, p. 182, fig. 106.

On the building in VII 5.14–15

Pompei 1748–1980. I tempi della documentazione (Rome, 1981), pp. 36–37; R. Angelone, "L'agenzia di un lanista in Pompei all'insegna di un famoso combattimento gladiatorio," *Atti Accademia Pontaniana*, n.s. 38 (1989) (Naples, 1990); G. Bechi, "Relazione degli scavi di Pompei," *Real Museo Borbonico* 1 (1824), pp. 5ff.; Della Corte, *Case ed abitanti*, p. 173; Fiorelli, *Descrizione di Pompei*, p. 236; Fröhlich, *Lararien und Fassadenbilder*, p. 326; Helbig, *Die Wandgemälde*, 1513; Schefold, *Die Wände Pompejis*, p. 189.

On the House of C. Holconius Rufus (VIII 4.4)

G. Fiorelli, *GdS* (1861), pp. 43–45; G. Minervini, "Scavamenti di Pompei," *Bullettino Archeologico Italiano* 1 (1862), pp. 50–51; Overbeck and Mau, *Pompeji in seinen Gebäuden*, p. 293; Schefold, *Die Wände Pompejis*, p. 223.

On the House of the Red Walls (VIII 5, 37)

A. Man, *BdI* 1884, pp. 16-21; F. Niccolini, *Le case e i monumenti di Pompei disegnati e descritti* IV, p. 20, pl. V; G.K. Boyce, *Corpus of the Lararia of Pompei, MemAmAc* 14, 1937, p. 77 pl. 31, 1-2; T. Fröhlich, *Lararien und fassadenbilder*, cit. pp. 92-93, 205, 291-292, 296.

On the House of the Sculptor (VIII 7.24)

PPM 8 (1998), pp. 718ff; G. Fiorelli, *PAH* 1, 2, pp. 63, 70–71; idem, *La Descrizione di Pompei* (Naples, 2001), p. 357; A. Maiuri, "Una nuova pittura nilotica a Pompei," *Mem. Linc.*, ser. 8, vol. 7 (1957), pp. 65–80; Overbeck and Mau, *Pompeji in seinen Gebäuden*, pp. 281–82.

On the shop in IX 3.13

G. K. Boyce, "Corpus of Lararia of Pompeii," *Memoirs of the American Academy in Rome* 14 (1937), no. 411, 2; Fiorelli, *Descrizione di Pompei*, p. 395; Sogliano, *Le pitture murali campane*, n. 668.

On the thermopolium (IX 8.8)

A. Sogliano, *NSc* (1899), p. 126; idem, "Il primitivo ludo gladiatorio di Pompei," *Rendiconti Real Accademia dei Lincei* 30 (1921), nos. 1–3, pp. 24–25; G. Spano, *Alcune osservazioni nascenti da una descrizione dell'Anfiteatro di Pompei* (Salerno, 1952), p. 50.

On the tavern in IX 9.8

PPM 3 (1986), p. 553; Croisille, *Poésie et art figuré de Néron aux Flaviens*, p. 263; A. Mau, *RM* (1889), pp. 27–31; Schefold, *Die Wände Pompejis*, p. 282; A. Sogliano, *NSc* (1887), pp. 563–64; idem, *NSc* (1889), p. 126.

On the tavern in IX 12.7

M. Della Corte, *NSc* (1912), pp. 442ff.; idem, *Case ed abitanti*, p. 323; Felletti Maj, *La tradizione italica*, pp. 332ff., figs. 163–64; Fröhlich, *Lararien und Fassadenbilder*, F71, p. 339, fig. 58,2; Schefold, *Die Wände Pompejis*, p. 289; V. Spinazzola, *Pompei alla luce degli scavi nuovi* 1, pp. 170ff., figs. 211–12, pls. 4, 63.

On the Suburban Baths

S. De Caro, "La città imperiale," *Pompei* 2, F. Zevi, ed. (Naples, 1992), pp. 11–38; L. Jacobelli, "Vicende edilizie ed interventi pittorici nelle Terme Suburbane a Pompei," *Mededelingen van het Nederlands Instituut te Rome* 54 (1995), pp. 154–65.

On the Tomb of Umbricius Scaurus

S. Adamo Muscettola, "La cultura figurativa privata in età imperiale," *Pompei* 2, F. Zevi, ed. (1992), pp. 111–12; F. M. Avellino, *Atti della Società Pontaniana di Napoli* 3 (1819), pp. 193–210; F. Coarelli, "Il rilievo con scene gladiatorie," p. 97, pl. 42; H. Döhl and P. Zanker, "La scultura," *Pompei 79* (Naples, 1979), p. 188, fig. 97; G. Fiorelli, *PAH* 1, 3, 93; F. Mazois, *Les ruines de Pompéi* (Paris, 1824–38), pp. 46–51, pl. 31; H. Mielsch, *Römische Stuckreliefs* (Heidelberg, 1975), p. 184, no. A6; A. L. Millin de Grandmaison, *Description des tombeaux qui ont été découverts à Pompei dans l'année 1812* (Paris, 1813), pp. 10–68, pl. 3; F. Niccolini, *Le case ed i monumenti di Pompei, disegnati e descritti* 1 (Naples, 1854); Overbeck and Mau, *Pompeji in seinen Gebäuden*, p. 420, fig. 222; P. Sabbatini Tumolesi, *Gladiatorum paria. Annunci di spettacoli gladiatorii a Pompei* (Rome, 1980), pp. 62ff.; V. Kockel, *Die Grabbauten vor dem Herkulaner Tor in Pompeiji* (Mainz am Rhein, 1983), pp. 75ff.

On the Tomb of Vestorius Priscus

Pompei oltre la vita (Pompei, 1998), pp. 45–49; J. M. Dentzer, "La tombe de C. Vestorius dans la tradition de la peinture italique," *Mélanges de l'Ecole Française de Rome* 74 (1962), pp. 533–94; S. T. A. M. Mols and E .M. Moormann, "Ex parvo crevit," *Riv. Studi Pomp.* 6 (1993–94); G. Spano, "La tomba dell'edile C. Vestorio Prisco in Pompei," *Mem. Linc.* 7, 3 (1943), pp. 237–315.

On the marble relief from the necropolis at the Stabian Gate

Pompei oltre la vita, pp. 33–35; Döhl and Zanker, "La scultura," pp. 188–89; B. Maiuri, "Rilievo gladiatorio di Pompei," *Rendiconti Accademia dei Lincei*, ser. 8, vol. 2 (1947), nos. 11–12 (1948), pp. 491–510; A. Varone, "I giochi e gli spettacoli," *Bellezza e lusso*, p. 180, n. 28.

On Tomb 2 EN in the necropolis at the Nucerian Gate

A. D'Ambrosio and S. De Caro, "La necropoli di Porta Nocera," *Un impegno per Pompei* (Milan, 1983).

On the representations of gladiators in various materials

N. Castiglione Morelli Del Franco, "Le lucerne della casa di Giulio Polibio," *Pompei, Herculaneum, Stabiae* 1 (1983), pp. 213–58; A. Maiuri, "All'insegna del gladiatore," *Pompei ed Ercolano: Fra case ed abitanti* (Florence, 1983), pp. 62–65; O. Elia, "La scultura pompeiana in tufo," *Cronache Pompeiane* 1 (1975), pp. 134–35; S. Ciro Nappo, "Regio I insula 20," *Rivista Studi Pompeiani* 2 (1988), pp. 186–92; A. Levi, *Le terracotte figurate del Museo Nazionale di Napoli* (Florence, 1926); H. von Rohden, *Die Terracotten von Pompeji* (Stuttgart, 1880); J. B. Ward-Perkins and A. Claridge, *Pompei A.D. 79* (Boston, 1978).

ABBREVIATIONS

Note: Throughout the text, buildings from Pompeii are indicated by region, *insula* (block), and building number. Thus, "III 2.1" is region 3, block 2, building 1.

ADS	Archivio Disegni della Soprintendenza Archeologica di Napoli
BdI	*Bullettino dell'Instituto di Correspondenza Archeologica*
CIL	*Corpus Inscriptionum Latinarum*
DAIR	Deutsches Archaeologisches Institut Rom
GdS	*Giornale degli scavi di Pompei*, Napoli
Mem. Linc.	Atti della reale Academia Nazionale dei Lincei. Memorie della classe di scienze morali, storiche e filologiche, Roma
NSc	Atti della reale Acc. Nazionale dei Lincei. Notizie degli Scavi di Antichità, Roma
PAH	G. Fiorelli, *Pompeianarum Antiquitatum Historia*, 2 vols. (Naples, 1860–1862)
PPM	*Pompei. Pitture e Mosaici*
RM	Mitteilungen des Deutschen Archaeologischen Instituts. Römische Abteilung.Rom.Berlin, etc.

INDEX